To my adored late father, Robert Fairs Hendry,
my inspirational mother, Ina, and my courageous son, Daniel.
You have all taught me to give voices to
those who are silent. Thank you.

SHARON HENDRY

RADHIKA'S STORY

SURVIVING
HUMAN TRAFFICKING

NEW
HOLLAND

Published in 2010 by New Holland Publishers (UK) Ltd
London • Cape Town • Sydney • Auckland
www.newhollandpublishers.com
Garfield House, 86–88 Edgware Road, London W2 2EA,
United Kingdom
80 McKenzie Street, Cape Town 8001, South Africa
Unit 1, 66 Gibbes Street, Chatswood, NSW 2067, Australia
218 Lake Road, Northcote, Auckland, New Zealand

10 9 8 7 6 5 4 3 2 1

A catalogue record for this book is available from the British Library

ISBN 978 184773 725 0

Publisher:	Aruna Vasudevan
Editor:	Scala Quin
Inside Design:	2M design
Cover Design:	Madeline Meckiffe
Production:	Melanie Dowland

Reproduction by Pica Digital Pte. Ltd, Singapore
Printed and bound in India by Replika Press
The paper used to produce this book is sourced from sustainable forests.

'Human trafficking crosses cultures and continents....
All of us have a responsibility to bring
this practice to an end....Through partnerships,
we can confront it head-on and lift its victims
from slavery to freedom.'
–Hillary Clinton, US Secretary of State, 2010

Contents

List of Illustrations

Plate section 1

1. Radhika carrying Rohan © Manish Koirala.
2. Radhika's mother, Maiya Phuyal, at home
   © Manish Koirala.
3. Radhika's father, Ramprasad Phuyal © Manish Koirala.
4. Radhika's paternal grandmother, Hari Prem
   © Manish Koirala.
5. Radhika's family outside their home in Kavresthali
   © Manish Koirala.
6. The Balaju vegetable market where Radhika's trafficking
   nightmare began © Manish Koirala.
7. Chennai train station. Courtesy of Alamy (dbimages).
8. Radhika reveals the scar left after her kidney was forcibly
   removed in a Chennai hospital © Manish Koirala.
9. Sindhupalchowk. Courtesy of Corbis (Macduff Everton).
10. Krishna 'Purne' Pariyar, one of the men who trafficked
    Radhika © Maiti Nepal.
11. Rohan and Radhika outside her family home
    © Manish Koirala.

Plate section 2

1. Lakshmi. Courtesy of iStockphoto (Jaya Kumar).
2. Train. Courtesy of Flickr (Yamagota Hiroo).
3. The jail © Manish Koirala.
4. The Maiti Nepal refuge © Manish Koirala.

5. Maiti Nepal founder, Anuradha Koirala © Manish Koirala.
6. Radhika and other girls at the refuge making beaded bracelets in the Maiti Nepal workshop © Manish Koirala.
7. Radhika, Rohan and other child survivors of human trafficking © Manish Koirala.
8. Radhika and Rohan with her family in their native village © Manish Koirala.
9. Radhika and Rohan with Radhika's grandmother and father outside the family home © Manish Koirala.
10. Radhika's father, Ramprasad, with Rohan © Manish Koirala.
11. Radhika's youngest sister, Nani Maiya, with Rohan © Manish Koirala.
12. Rohan with Radhika and her mother © Manish Koirala.
13. The author, Radhika's 102-year-old grandmother, Hari Prem, and translator, Elisha Shrestha © Manish Koirala.
14. Radhika with Rohan © Manish Koirala.

Acknowledgements

I would like to thank *The Sun* and its three successive editors – David Yelland, Rebekah Brooks (now CEO of News International) and Dominic Mohan – for giving me the opportunity to do the job of my dreams every single day.

I am also indebted to my co-pilot Elisha Shrestha, of Maiti Nepal, translator, fixer and Nepalese history and language expert extraordinaire – I couldn't have done it without you.

Thanks also goes to my publisher, Aruna Vasudevan: your patience with a novice author has been exemplary.

Anuradha Koirala needs a very special mention also for welcoming me into her wonderful shelter and allowing me to witness an inspirational legend at work.

Finally and most importantly, I would like to extend my heartfelt gratitude to Radhika herself. Your story moved me to tears when you first shared it with me, sitting cross-legged on a lawn outside Maiti Nepal on a humid July afternoon in 2009. I will *never* forget your courage and dignity or the extraordinary love you possess for Rohan. My wish is that one day he will read your story and know this, too.

Foreword
Joanna Lumley

At first you might think that you are hearing a story from a desperate writer of soap operas; there is too much horror here, too many cruelties and indignities, rampant injustice, almost unbelievable courage ... and yet it is all true, every word of it; and not only true of Radhika, but of thousands of women and girls like her.

In an age where we congratulate ourselves that slavery has been overthrown and that women have rights which are upheld, these stark facts stare us in the face: many women have never been more abused than they are today, right now, this minute, in this tiny world across which we can email in an instant. And yet, this is not a story from another century, although it feels as though it comes from the Dark Ages. This testimony carries a message that will ring true for all time; that bravery and love can counterbalance the nightmares contained within it.

Nepal and India, where Radhika's story takes place, are places of extremes. Beauty and disease, desperate poverty and a surfeit of riches, hunger and excess jostle with each other, making life for their peoples a constant struggle. All manner of criminal activities thrive, not least enforced prostitution and the trafficking of women and children.

The damage and destruction caused by these activities are almost beyond description, and no one writes of them with more compassion and insight than Sharon Hendry.

She and I visited Maiti Nepal together during the rainy season in July 2009. Maiti Nepal: the word 'maiti' means 'mother', 'mother's home', 'mother's love', a 'sanctuary' and 'protector'. There, we saw children with HIV/AIDs and venereal diseases, girls with hips dislocated from brutal sexual abuse as seven year olds, young women whose minds had been forever scarred by what they had endured, all being brought back slowly and carefully into a world in which people can be trusted, where skills are taught, where music and dancing happen every day, where broken lives are fixed. The extraordinary and charismatic powerhouse behind the home, Mrs Anuradha Koirala, asked if I would help spread the word of their work in the United Kingdom. I said 'yes' in a heartbeat.

I felt that this story, just one of the many – too many – which are waiting untold in dumb silence, must be heard; and if her story prevents even one more child being sold into this appalling slavery, brave Radhika will not have suffered in vain.

Joanna Lumley is Goodwill Ambassador for Maiti Nepal, an organization that helps victims of human trafficking. A celebrated actor, she is an acknowledged human rights campaigner.

Preface

The train carriage door slammed shut and Radhika Phuyal instantly felt the intense heat closing in on her.

Her new emerald green kurta salwar, the long tunic over loose trousers that girls of her age traditionally wear, stuck uncomfortably to her skin and her long, glossy black hair weighed heavy on her back. Her breathing came in unusually short and shallow bursts as a terrible and sudden fear of the unknown, of what lay ahead of her on this exciting journey, began to overwhelm her.

The creeping unease she was feeling at the prospect of an unfamiliar train journey was tempered only by the fact that she was going on holiday for the first time in her life.

'H-O-L-I-D-A-Y', she whispered to herself over and over again. Radhika liked the feel of the letters rolling over her tongue like exotic, sumptuous fruits. Long gone were the days of eking out an impoverished existence selling spinach on the dusty roadsides of Kathmandu.

The Hindu gods finally appeared to be giving Radhika some respite from the relentlessness of her life. Her offerings had paid off: she had always made a point of giving sweet milk and rice to Lakshmi, the goddess of wealth and prosperity, whenever she visited the temple.

Lakshmi was her favourite, not just because she was the most beautiful of the gods, but because she stood for purity and fertility. Radhika was certain that Lakshmi had had a hand in helping to transport her from her place among the teeming mass of humanity who sold vegetables alongside Kathmandu's Biṣhnumati River to the life of luxury that the people travelling with her on this journey – her 'new family' – had promised awaited her in a far off land.

Her life had changed so radically in just a matter of weeks, making the seemingly unattainable believable. Before that Radhika's dreams had appeared to be well beyond her reach – a family debt had forced her prematurely out of the school she loved so much and into work, first harvesting, then later selling her family's vegetable produce.

After that, she quickly recognized that it would take a miracle to save her from the poverty that had already swallowed up the hopes and dreams of thousands of other uneducated Nepalese girls like her.

'Perhaps this is it…. My miracle!,' Radhika thought to herself, sinking back into her seat as the train left the station, gathering speed to only the gods knew where. 'Perhaps this is finally my sign from goddess Lakshmi that things are going to change.'

She listened to the soft, rhythmic whirring of the train against the track, feeling like the heroine of one of the epic Bollywood films that she had seen advertised so often on posters around Kathmandu.

Finally, Radhika Phuyal was going somewhere. Exactly where she didn't yet know – her new family hadn't told her the destination yet. But that didn't matter. When you're born into poverty in the fourth poorest country in the world, it is sometimes just enough to *go*.

Anyway, the element of mystery about the whole journey only added to her excitement and made the sense of adventure all the more poignant. For the first time, Radhika truly felt that something momentous was going to happen, something that might change her life forever.

Now all she had to do was to cast her worries aside and enjoy the ride. As the sacred Hindu text the Bhagavad Gita teaches: 'There is neither this world nor the world beyond nor happiness for the one who doubts.'

And at that point, Radhika knew that she should not have any doubts – she really shouldn't have a care in the world. She was, after all, on the first of hopefully many journeys to the rest of her life.

What on earth did she have to worry about?

The sterile smell of hospital disinfectant jolted Radhika out of a deep sleep. She vomited.

A man's face began to swim into view. She concentrated, trying to bring him into focus. Who was he? Murari Pariyar! *That* was it. The friend of the family she worked for. He'd appeared at the station and had been introduced to Radhika before she got on the train. But where was everyone else? And *where* was she?

Gradually, Radhika became aware of another presence in the room, another man who was dressed in white.

She tried to focus, but it was *so* hard. *So* confusing. She struggled to concentrate and then realization struck. The man was a doctor. But *what* was a doctor doing here?

Had she been in some kind of accident?

As Radhika became more awake, she began to feel a terrible sense of doom, a growing sense of fear. Then the questions came hard and fast.

Where was she?

What was she doing here?

What was wrong with her?

Why was she lying in a hospital bed?

What had happened to her in the time since she'd got on the train to her great new life?

Where was the goddess Lakshmi now?

How had she come to this?

THE CORRUPTION
OF
INNOCENCE

Beginnings

SOUTH Asia is at the heart of an international trade in human organs. The equation is simple but brutal. Take a donor pool of desperately poor people, a racket of ruthless human traffickers and a corrupt monitoring system and the outcome is a booming market in body parts. But with such a group of people to choose from, what led Radhika Phuyal, a young Nepalese girl, to become involved in this dangerous and illegal game? The answer is simple – a rural upbringing, a lack of education and, most importantly, an absence of any financial independence made her the perfect victim for the criminals involved in this multimillion dollar illegal market.

In a world in which, according to the World Health Organization (WHO), at least 10 percent of all transplants result from 'medical tourists' – that is those people from developed countries who obtain vitally needed organs from private transactions conducted in poor nations – some amount of illegal activity is perhaps not surprising. These travellers seek out local agents who 'source' kidneys, in any number of ways, and arrange for the transplants to take place. At least 15,000 kidneys are trafficked in this way each year and India is a particularly popular destination, with its steady and readily available source of harvestable organs. Nepal supplies many of the young girls whose organs are removed and redistributed – willingly or not.

Thus, Radhika found herself lying in a strange hospital room in a different country, largely because of her family circumstances, but also because she had continued to hold onto the dream of being something other than what she seemed fated to be.

One of six children, Radhika was born to humble yet high-caste Brahmin farmers in Kavresthali, a small country province 7km (4.3 miles) north-west of Kathmandu, Nepal's capital. The area is only an hour by bumpy road from the bustling city, but first-time visitors to Kavresthali could be forgiven for thinking that they had been teleported back centuries to a forgotten time, when agriculture was the mainstay of most families' fortunes. Whereas in Kathmandu, ancient, smog-spitting cars sit snarled in traffic jams for hours on end, tethered nose to bumper like braying donkeys, in Kavresthali, an almost spiritual silence prevails in the steppes overshadowed by the mighty Himalayas. Only the sound of laughter emanates from children playing hide and seek among a cluster of humble, whitewashed single storey houses built on the edge of the village. All around them, their parents and grandparents are bent double in the fields, sowing pumpkin and spinach seeds that will provide sustenance for their families and hopefully turn over a small profit at the local market.

Kavresthali is one of the largest villages in the Kathmandu District and has a population of approximately 7,000 inhabitants. Most are involved in small-scale farming businesses and each morning, soon after sunrise, women in brightly coloured saris emerge from the hillsides, carefully balancing hay baskets laden with vegetables on their backs. Possessing all the effortless elegance of prima ballerinas and with great poise, they walk into the city each day to sell the produce. If they are lucky, they will be accompanied by an equally industrious husband, brother or father, who will join them to sell milk. A man with several chickens strung around his neck represents one of the most entrepreneurial Kavresthali families – one which has its own poultry farm.

Here, there are none of the cosmopolitan cafes or stores selling modern pop music that now populate Kathmandu. Instead, Kavresthali's inhabitants are serious about the business of survival and often sow seeds in the roughly ploughed endless fields until their hands bleed.

To most outsiders who visit in the tourist season between September and November, life in Kavresthali might appear idyllic. The morning chill is soon eclipsed by a burning red sun that sets off the shades of green in the lush foothills against the cloying brown mud of the surrounding fields. The landscape is biblical in appearance and instills a sense of tranquillity in its visitors. Yet in the monsoon season, between June and August, the area is prone to landslides and most tourists would not welcome the reality of living in the village then with its limited electricity and water supply.

The only luxury afforded to local residents is a small shop, which forms the hub of village life. Selling everything from candles to crisps, it sits on a small dirt track between the fields and hillside.

Radhika's family – the Phuyals – is typical of the region's people. Five members, spanning three generations, live under one roof in a tight-knit example of traditional extended kinship. It is an affectionate arrangement in which love and stability are a given, but it also lends itself to an insular environment in which children are shielded from the gritty realities of the world outside Kavresthali.

Hari Prem, Radhika's 102-year-old grandmother, is a regular fixture outside the Phuyal family home, where she sits cross-legged, soaking up the sun. She is the head of the Phuyal family and dictates the rules that govern it. Nepalese women have few rights outside the home even though they are integral to the family structure.

Buddhist and Hindu women have tremendous influence on the welfare of tribes and especially their children. Women are involved in the seasonal harvests as well as the maintenance of small family farms. They are responsible for the cooking of their traditional, twice daily meals of *dhal bat* (rice and lentils) and for teaching and caring for the children of their village. Their cooperative methods of raising children contribute to the prosperity of a tribe and at times the very survival of a family depends on them.

The Phuyals' house sits high up on a lush green hillside and visitors require a certain level of fitness to trek the steep 2km (1.2 miles) pathway that leads up to its entrance from the centre of the village. The two-storey, three-room mud house is covered by a tin roof and outside, corn hangs drying on a small wooden porch area. This area also serves as a family gathering point where stories of old are passed down to new generations and gossip is chewed over alongside the sugar cane. A small raised platform doubles up as a seat by day and a bed by night.

Inside the house the ceilings are no more than 1.2m (4ft) high and it is necessary to crouch down to enter. Darkness prevails due to an absence of electricity and the walls are burnished with smoke from endless wood fires. Downstairs, the main communal area measures around 3.6m by 3.3m (12ft by 11ft) and is used as a dining area. A small wooden staircase leads upstairs where two small compartments contain ledges used as beds. As is her due as matriarch, Hari Prem has the pick of the rooms and has a view overlooking the valley. Radhika's mother, father, brother and sister share the remaining room and the ledge outside.

The house is devoid of any furniture or other decorative adornments. The Phuyals use small wooden blocks as chairs. The only luxuries they allow themselves are a small array of cooking pots and utensils and several wool blankets that serve to shield them from cold winter mornings and nights.

Two goats and a cow live adjacent to the communal living room in a small stable. They provide the Phuyals with milk, cheese and yoghurt and are well tended. Most of Kavresthali's inhabitants keep at least one cow or goat. The fact that the Phuyals have three animals sets their status slightly above that of the average village family.

A single standpipe outside in the yard provides water from the mountains for the entire household and a small spinach patch forms the staple ingredient for the most common meal – *dhal bat*.

Despite its humble lifestyle, Radhika's family comes from the highest level of the Hindu caste system. The Phuyals are Brahmins, the priestly caste, who are believed to have emerged from the mouth of Brahma, the revered Hindu god of creation. Below them in the system lie the Kshatriyas, the warrior or ruling class who were made from Brahma's arms.

The Vaishyas are merchants or artisans, who came from Brahma's thighs and the lowest caste – the Shudras – are unskilled labourers and servants who emerged from Brahma's feet. Finally, the Untouchables, the lowest of the low in terms of traditional Hindu society, lie outside of the caste system. Members of the upper castes consider the lower castes to be ritually unclean – although the great spiritual leader Mahatma Gandhi thought otherwise, referring to them as 'harijan', that is the 'children of God'.

Marrying someone from a different caste is social suicide and leads to severe repercussions, including being cut off from the family – a cruel blow in a society in which family and caste are so central to survival.

As Brahmins, the Phuyals are extremely proud of their bloodline. While several other families in Kavresthali belong to the same caste, the Phuyals are different, marked out as special because of their matriarch, Hari Prem.

This remarkable woman stands less than 1.2m (4ft) tall, but what she lacks in stature, Hari Prem certainly makes up for in spirit. Respected by the Phuyals and other villagers because of her age and experience, Hari Prem's face is shrivelled from over a century of life under the Nepalese sun – but each crevice tells a unique story. Her piercing blue eyes still flash with a spirit that makes her appear much younger and more mischievous than her actual years.

Unlike Radhika, her gentle-natured granddaughter, Hari Prem is direct and feisty. She is always at the centre of family discussions, laying down rules about everything from long-term financial planning to lunch menus and cajoling anyone who disagrees with her into changing his or her mind. She is especially forthright when it comes to her role in the Phuyal family – quite simply, without her it would fall apart.

Hari Prem gave birth to six children but only three survived. Her second-born child is Radhika's father Ramprasad, now aged 65. A gentle and retiring man, Ramprasad revealed a love of the land from an early age, which naturally led him to become a farmer. Hari Prem was always important to her son's life and as Ramprasad reached manhood, she continued to orchestrate most of the important matters in his life, including his marriage to Radhika's mother, Maiya.

A local beauty from good Brahmin stock, Maiya was – and is – perfect for Ramprasad in every way. The couple work the land together and run their small household harmoniously with an inherent closeness. Despite the years and harsh way of life, Maiya's beauty is still evident in her chiselled cheekbones and chocolate-brown eyes. With great dignity, she makes the journey back and forth from the fields to her home and completes the seemingly endless household chores without complaint.

Radhika has inherited her mother's slim frame and striking bone structure, but it is her father she resembles most in character. The pair share the same trusting nature and love nothing more than sitting side by side, cross-legged in the sun outside the family home, shaving sugar cane.

Parvati Khatiwada, aged 35, is the first-born daughter and possesses great beauty inherited from her mother, Maiya. She waved goodbye to her rural upbringing after entering into an arranged marriage with Sri Ram Khatiwada, the owner of a bag factory, three years older than her. Parvati now lives a more cosmopolitan life in central Kathmandu. Always perfectly groomed, she favours bright red kurtas, which are especially striking against her pale brown skin and glossy, long black hair. She prides herself on her impeccable manners and carries herself with great poise, gliding through Kathmandu's streets with enviable elegance in small kitten heels, her arms hidden by layers of colourful bangles.

Nine years older than Radhika, Parvati was not close to her younger sister when they were children. Since Radhika's experiences in India that has changed, however, and the two women have an extremely good relationship. Today Parvati plays a pivotal role in her sister's life and is largely responsible for Radhika and her son, Rohan, living at the Maiti Nepal refuge in Kathmandu. She visits them there almost every week and continues to help shield them from harm's way.

Sabita (Rimal) is the second eldest daughter and at 29, is just three years older than Radhika. She married a farmer and lives near to the family home, maintaining a similar lifestyle to the one into which she was born.

Radhika's younger sister, Nani Maiya Phuyal, is six years her junior and lives at the Phuyal family home with her parents. She voices 'modern' notions about remaining unmarried for the foreseeable future. Whether Radhika's experiences have had anything to do with Nani's attitude to marriage is debatable.

Radhika's brother, Balkrishna Phuyal, is the baby of the family at 15. Despite this he is old beyond his years; he gracefully bears the weight of his responsibilities as the sole son and heir to the family farm. But Balkrishna was not always the only son. The Phuyals had an older son, Radhakrishna who was 11 years older than Parvati. Despite the age difference between Radhika and her eldest brother, Radhakrishna is the person whose absence arguably had the most impact on Radhika and what would happen to her later in life. It is Radhakrishna who ignites the most fierce emotions in the young woman – and about whom she feels the most guilt.

'Radhakrishna … cherished me,' Radhika recalls. 'He used to take me everywhere with him in the reed basket we used for grass cuttings to feed our animals. I worshipped him and in turn, he adored me. One day, when he was 27 and I was around 7, we went to the top of a hill together to cut grass. He stumbled and fell off the edge of a crevice and died. I ran home to tell my father but he didn't believe me so I had to drag him to the hillside. I was so traumatized by what I had witnessed, I blanked out the experience from an early age.

'After my brother was cremated I felt like my belief in anything spiritual had died. Of course his death wasn't my fault but I couldn't help thinking I could have done something to stop him from falling.

'Afterwards, I wanted to make things better for my family, to make up for what had happened. Before the accident, we were a happy family and there was light and laughter in the house. But then it stopped. My mother went on to have more children but after losing his first-born son, my father wasn't interested in life for a very long time.'

This may go some way to explaining why no one took a proper interest in Radhika's education. At the age of 10, her schooling effectively stopped, even though she dreamed of carrying on with her education.

'I felt so proud each morning skipping down the hillside in my uniform – a sky-blue shirt and skirt. But my elder sisters had left home to get married, my mother was suffering from heart disease and my father was struggling to maintain the farm. Suddenly, the burden fell on me to help out and I had to quit my studies.

'I was helping my mother with household chores and working alongside my father on our farm. I was just too busy to concentrate [on school work]. Luckily, I had learned to read ... [W]henever I found an old newspaper lying around in the village, I would study all the pages and read about famous Indian actors and actresses who appeared in Bollywood films. I found them captivating.'

Just four short years later, aged 14, Radhika found herself selling spinach on a busy Kathmandu roadside to help support her high-caste but extremely impoverished family. A good-looking girl all alone in the city, Radhika was the perfect target for human traffickers trained to seek out uneducated and unsuspecting victims.

But how did she get to that point?

The same ancient marriage tradition that has dictated and directed Nepalese women's lives for centuries, ultimately forced Radhika into an unnervingly modern world. Even today, a girl is expected to enter into an arranged marriage with a suitable candidate as soon as both her family and the prospective groom's agree. But marriage isn't a simple issue. The girls, in particular, have to tick a long list of boxes before they are deemed acceptable for wedlock. Their suitability is not just based on where families fit into the caste system – one of the main factors that the Phuyals had to consider – it also relates to other matters such as social standing, profession, name, the paleness of skin, beauty and even age.

Of course, a good marriage – the ultimate aim of every family with daughters – comes at a huge price, well beyond what the girl's family (who usually foots the bill) can afford. The dowry, the money and possessions given to a bridegroom's family by the bride's family, are the most pressing issues. It is essential that the bride's family doesn't lose face. In many cases, the bride's family incurs huge debts to cover the dowry, sometimes leaving them financially destitute, as in the case of Radhika's family.

Even today, the matter of the dowry is a serious business, not just in South Asian countries, but in countries with high numbers of immigrants from those areas. The prospective husband's family first discusses the details of the dowry that the bride's family can afford, and only then in most cases will they progress to the next step, the woman herself. The dowry is called *daijo* in Nepal and *dahej* in India and the deal is non-negotiable. In traditional communities, a marriage will not take place until the financial discussions are finalized.

A family's status is thought to be boosted in society if it can bequeath a large dowry. If it is financially weak and cannot afford the amount, many families take out loans and sometimes mortgage their land and property. There are numerous examples of a wealthy father becoming impoverished after paying dowries to the families of all his daughters' prospective husbands. More seriously, many women have to endure terrible mental and physical torture if their families fail to hand over their promised dowries, or the amount demanded by their husbands' families. In extreme cases, women have been burned alive in retribution for unpaid dowries. The dowry is, therefore, of ulitmate importance in marriage settlements.

In Radhika's case, her family was particularly financially vulnerable. The Phuyals eked out a humble existence, working hard as Himalayan hill farmers to grow such crops as spinach, peas and pumpkins on their collective farm land. Their livelihood and well-being owed much to the elements and how well a crop would perform annually. They worked hard to support Radhika and her siblings, but they were also aware of how important it was to settle Parvati, their first-born daughter, well, especially in a family with several daughters and only one son. Parvati was beautiful and a rare prize, but good looks alone can't guarantee a good marriage partner. Money, in most cases, matters. And it was that issue that brought undue stress on the Phuyal family.

'My parents were forced to take out a loan from a village collective to finance my sister Parvati's dowry when she entered into an arranged marriage,' Radhika recalls.

'A lot of financial problems arose at home and when my mother and father couldn't afford to pay back the money they had borrowed, the collective threatened to take our home.

'We are humble people but respected members of the highest Brahmin caste in Hindu society and I couldn't bear to see my parents struggling and humiliated like that. So I left our village on foot when I was just 14 and walked for three hours to the nearest bus station.

'I boarded a bus for Kathmandu and rented a room in Khusibu, in the Balaju district of the city, for 500 Nepalese Rupees (NPR; about £4.50) per week. I began selling the family produce … along the riverside.

'I was making 1,000 NPR (about £9.00) per week and, of course, sending the profit home, so everything began to settle down and was normal. Life seemed perfect to me.'

There are few places in Kathmandu that better demonstrate the juxtaposition of beauty and poverty than Balaju. Formerly a small village to the north of Kathmandu, it is now an established industrial suburb of the Nepalese capital. Balaju's Mahendra Park is popular with townspeople who can afford the luxury of picnics and leisure time. But for most, it is a densely populated, concrete dustbowl that attracts a melting pot of Nepalese people in search of a better life.

Here, each morning hundreds of traders dressed in brightly coloured kurtas set up stalls alongside the Bishnumati River. After gently pressing their hands together and uttering the traditional Hindu greeting 'Namaste' (which literally means: 'I bow to you'), they go to war with one another, competing ferociously to sell an array of wares, ranging from donkeys to dish cloths. On large, reed mats under the open sky, a rainbow of succulent fruits and perfectly grown vegetables lie side by side, waiting to be scrutinized by discerning customers.

It was to here that Radhika gravitated after arriving in the city. Her natural beauty and quiet manner immediately attracted attention from stall holders and customers alike. Small in height and slight in stature, Radhika stood just 5ft 4ins (1.64m) tall and weighed less than 8 stone (50.8kg). Her shoulder-length glossy black hair was immaculately groomed and usually pinned back into a neat ponytail. Naturally good looking, she had inherited her mother's striking bone structure and her father's warm brown eyes – a combination that made her beauty, even then, interesting rather than classic. She had no need for make-up – her young, olive-coloured skin still flawless and unlined even after exposure to the strong Nepalese sun.

Radhika's looks, age and gentle manner undoubtedly helped set her apart from the other more experienced and aggressive vendors and she began to attract a regular clientele. After about six months of working in Balaju,

Radhika began to notice one customer, an attractive man in his mid-30s, who seemed particularly intent on establishing a rapport with her and despite the obvious age difference, she was strangely drawn to him. At 36 years of age, the man, Sanjay Lama, was about the age that her beloved brother, Radhakrishna, would have been, had he lived.

Radhika recalls, 'A dark and handsome Nepalese man approached me one day on the vegetable stall after he had been watching me for some time. He engaged me in some polite conversation, which gave me the impression he was from a well-off family. Initially, he would come at the same time each day – around lunch time – and stay for a while, simply talking about the weather or the price of things at the market. Then, after a few weeks, he began asking me how long I was planning to sell vegetables for – implying I was wasting my life. He presented himself as someone who was going to help me get a better job. He told me I should consider him to be "family" and trust him implicitly.'

Lama successfully presented himself to the young girl as a caring, big brother figure in an overwhelmingly unfamiliar cityscape, where she, in effect, had no one else to care for her. In reality, however, Lama was an experienced and well-known human trafficker on the look out for his next 'victim'. His engaging and caring manner were part of a 'grooming' technique that he executed professionally and precisely. He saw Radhika, his latest conquest in a line of many, as little more than a piece of flesh.

He had spent weeks scanning the bustling market scene for the most trusting country girl in town and once he had decided on the now 15-year-old Radhika as his number one target, he quickly succeeded in gaining the confidence of the innocent and naive country girl over the months that followed. While Lama pretended that he wanted to help Radhika out of her current situation, his real thoughts were on something else altogether – how well Radhika would fit as the supplier of the kidney he needed to fulfil the order from his next client.

Organ trafficking is big business in India and Nepal, where men like Lama work as part of a vast network that can involve hundreds of henchmen. The issue was forced into public consciousness in August 2008 after the arrest of an Indian surgeon, Amit Kumar, who became known as 'Dr Horror'. Kumar was believed to be the head of a criminal network that ran a multimillion dollar racket in kidneys from Gurgaon, in the northern Indian state of Haryana. He is believed to have 'stolen' more than 500 kidneys in 9 years.

Kumar's manhunt was triggered by a police raid on a Gurgaon clinic involved in illegal transplants. According to Indian authorities, a group of Kumar's henchmen were paid to prowl the poor markets of Old Delhi and Uttar Pradesh in search of potential 'donors'. Once selected, the victims were enticed into the traffickers' hands with false promises of well-paid jobs – and those who resisted were drugged and operated on anyway. The organs harvested from the 'donors' were bought for around US $1,000 (around £660) and then sold on to wealthy Indians or nonresident foreigners for up to US $30,000 (around £20,000).

Kumar was eventually found hiding out in Chitwan, a district famous for housing Nepal's most famous national park, after which he was deported back to India, where he was subsequently jailed. He was found to possess a number of different passports and many aliases. His property assets in Gurgaon, Mumbai and Canada alone were valued at tens of millions of rupees and he had at least 12 accounts at different banks scattered around the world. Although no direct links between Lama and Kumar have ever been established, it is certain that Lama was working for a similar organ trafficking 'godfather', and was paid to scour the poorest city suburbs for suitable 'donors' of lucrative body parts.

Radhika's youth and innocence made her particularly susceptible to Lama's experienced charm. Raised in the bosom of a close-knit family, in which every man she encountered had loved and cherished her, Radhika had no reason to believe that other men she came across would be any different. So, it wasn't difficult for Lama to lull this sexually naive and trusting girl into a false sense of security. He played up his 'big brother' role and offered this lonely girl, a caring shoulder to cry on.

Eventually, Lama told Radhika that he had found her a job as a housekeeper to a rich family in the city. Excited by the idea of such a radical change to her limited circumstances, a golden opportunity to achieve more than the hard existence she was eking out each day in the market, Radhika immediately fell in with his plans. She agreed to accompany Lama to Koteshwor, a busy business district to the east of Kathmandu.

'I was impressed when we arrived at a detached three-storey town house,' Radhika recalls. 'There were two cars and two bikes parked outside, which confirmed the wealth and status of the family who I later learned owned a furniture factory.

'Lama introduced me immediately to the husband, wife and three sons, who appeared to be in their mid- to late 20s. The youngest – Sanjay – appeared to be the [one] who took control of things and was [seemed] particularly close to his mother.

'I was overwhelmed by the splendour of their house. The huge rooms contained beautiful ornate furniture and I saw a television close-up for the first time.

'It was a million miles apart from the sort of home I had grown up in. In my lounge there was a mud floor and the occasional goat [would wander] in. [Now], I was walking on beautifully woven carpets.

'But most striking was the family's kindness. They invited me to sit with them and I hungrily devoured the freshly prepared dinner of rice, curry and *dhal* [lentils].

'I remember focussing mainly on the mother, who looked Mongolian in appearance. She was in her mid-40s and plump with fair skin. She had difficulty walking and [suffered from] a pronounced shortness of breath. I felt sorry for her and was determined to help her as much as possible.

'The family went off to sleep after dinner but not before showing me to my own private bedroom.

I had never slept in a proper bed before and felt as if I had gone to heaven.'

The next day, reality set in.

As the morning unfolded Radhika was to experience a series of rather odd and disturbing events, but so sophisticated was the web woven around her that it did not even occur to the young girl to challenge what happened to her. The first thing occurred at breakfast, which Radhika had been invited to eat with the family. Radhika was told to get ready for a ride into the city with the family and assumed that they were going shopping, perhaps to the market to buy vegetables. Instead, after a short trip, she was led into a strange modern building, a medical clinic as it turned out. Here, she was asked to give blood and urine samples. Alarm bells began to ring in her head at that point, but when she asked what the tests were for, the family reassured her that it was all routine and the checkup was just to make sure that she was fit enough to work for them. Radhika had no choice but to believe them. Why should she think otherwise?

'I'd never had a job interview before, let alone a proper "city job" and just told myself that must be what everyone had to do,' she says. 'After a few hours, I was relieved when the results came back and they told me: "Everything is normal – you can stay."'

Any lingering doubts she may have had were further erased when Radhika was taken on a shopping trip after the clinic visit. Not for vegetables but for clothes. For the first time in her life, it seemed to Radhika that she was being treated like the Bollywood stars she had so admired on screen. Her new 'family' took her to a series of small boutiques and treated her to two sets of finely tailored kurta salwar and *two* pairs of jeans.

Radhika had only ever seen jeans on the Bollywood movie stars gazing out from the torn pages of the second-hand gossip magazines she would sometimes find lying along the roadside near the market. Standing in front of the mirror in the boutique, she ran her hands over the smooth contours of her jean-clad hips, marvelling at the image of the stranger staring back at her and the softness of the deep blue denim. It was so different to anything she'd worn before. Surely this was a sign that she was moving up in the world?

And she didn't just have new clothes but cosmetics as well! For the first time in her life she had her own proper make-up. She loved the smell of the delicately scented citrus soaps and the luxurious shampoo made from coconut oil. Her new toiletries were a far cry from the basic kohl, cold water, henna paste and plain yoghurt she had used to pamper herself with previously.

How could she ever repay such kindness, though? She could reward her big-hearted employers with sheer hard work, but it hardly seemed enough to compensate them for such generosity. What else could she offer them? Radhika thought hard. She had nothing else to give them.

She returned to the family's impressive residence determined to scrub each room from top to bottom. But there was no time to do so – the family already had other plans. They were going on a trip and Radhika was to come with them.

'They asked me to pack my bags with everything they had just bought for me except for one particularly smart kurta salwar which they said I should wear immediately. They told me we were going on holiday together early the next morning ... somewhere in India – but [they] never told me the exact destination.'

Although India is just across the border from Nepal, to young girls like Radhika it is an exotic, far off country – another planet, really. It was a land that certainly inhabited Radhika's dreams. In her imagination, India was peopled with beautiful Bollywood heroines and handsome heroes, living in some of the most stunning scenery on earth, the landscapes that Radhika had stared at so adoringly on film posters. It never occured to the young girl that India might be similar to Nepal in many ways, that it might have a darker side to the one represented on celluloid, that it might suffer from some of the same social and economic problems as her native Nepal. But even if it had, would it have mattered? After all, Radhika Phuyal was going to India. Who would believe it?

Thus, as she clambered into an old Fiat taxi beside her new employers and their children at 7 a.m. one cold but sunny winter's morning, Radhika couldn't stop smiling. They got out at Naya Bus Park in Balaju, the main hub for buses making long journeys in and out of Kathmandu.

Radhika stared with growing wonder at the eclectic mix of locals and wide-eyed tourists fighting their way through stifling diesel fumes to climb on and off the crowded vehicles that were taking them to new horizons.

It was now almost two years since she had first left her small village to board the bus to Kathmandu and that experience had been very different to her current one. Then, she had been alone and afraid, fearful of just how she was going to make a living in the big city. Now, here she was, aged just 16, and about to embark on a much bigger journey, literally crossing new frontiers to *India*. She could barely contain her excitement.

Radhika watched as a man walked towards them, joining their small party. Introduced to her as a friend of her new employers, Murari Pariyar was in his mid-20s, around the same age as the sons of her employers. A short, lean man with long hair, he exchanged pleasantries with Radhika's employers. Soon after, the group, including Pariyar, boarded the bus. It seemed that Pariyar was coming with them. Once onboard the crowded, 30-seater vehicle Radhika absorbed every sight, every smell, every noise, cherishing every moment – even the discomfort of the bus was a pleasure.

She had a lot to take in. It was to be a gruelling 12 hours before the dated vehicle reached its destination of Birganj, in the Terai region of southern Nepal, which borders with India, but to Radhika it went by in a flash.

Birganj is a pleasant border town in southern Nepal, it lies 190km (118 miles) west of Kathmandu and just 2km (1.2 miles) north of the border of the Indian state of Bihar. Known as the gateway to Nepal, it has a population of just over 112,000 people, and its cigarette manufacturing, fish breeding and sugar industries make the town a major business centre in Nepal, one renowned for its trade with India.

When they arrived there, Radhika gazed out of the bus's scratched window, craning her neck to take in the teeming townscape in front of her. She soaked up its atmosphere of prosperity as confident businessmen strode along the town's dusty streets, while endless blue lorries shuttled cargo back and forth along the smog-filled roads. She could barely contain her excitement at being transported to this new place – the first of many, she hoped. In that moment, it felt to Radhika like the world was her oyster, ripe for picking. Anything was now possible, she thought to herself. *Anything*.

She followed the family as they disembarked from the bus and began to prepare for the next phase of the journey, the comparatively short 45-minute drive to the Indian border. Radhika's excitement grew as the minutes ticked by and the landscape whizzed past her.

Suddenly, amid the fleeting patchwork of paddy fields, her gaze fixed on what appeared to be a train station and a sign declaring 'BORDER'. They were almost there. India lay just beyond that sign.

Radhika boarded an old blue train and settled into a comfortable seat next to her female employer. The woman's husband shared the same carriage, while Pariyar and her sons sat in an adjoining section to the compartment.

Radhika looked around; she began to take in her surroundings. The carriage interior was pale blue. The colour made Radhika feel cool and calm because it somehow seemed to lower the temperature of the stuffy air inside. But it did nothing to rid the carriage of the stale curry smell that clung to the velour upholstery, worn down to the metal below in patches. She didn't care though – the journey on which she was about to embark was going to change her life. She just knew.

In a state of euphoria, believing that whatever happened next, whatever life threw at her, it would be worth it, Radhika knew that she was the luckiest girl in the world. Life just didn't get better than this.

'I don't remember who, but someone in the family offered me a mouth-wateringly cold drink of Coke. My throat was parched and my lips were dry so I devoured it greedily.

'I remember thinking how good it felt to drink because it was so cool and thirst-quenching.

'After that, I drifted off to sleep and lost consciousness for a very long time.'

A terrible awakening

RADHIKA'S eyelids felt heavy. She struggled to remember what had happened as she forced them open, rapidly blinking at the sudden brightness of the dazzling light.

The sun? That would make sense. She remembered now. She was on holiday with her new employers.

But as the glare faded and she became more accustomed to her surroundings, her gaze took in the whitewashed walls, she felt the highly starched sheets beneath her palms and inhaled the unmistakable smell of chemicals.

She forced herself to concentrate. Wherever she was, she wasn't on holiday. She wasn't sleeping on an Indian beach somewhere hot. The smells, noise, feel of the place made Radhika realize that she in a hospital.

But how? Why? Had she been in an accident?

All she could remember was being on the train with her new employers. What had happened to her since then?

If only she could she remember.

Out of the corner of her eye she glimpsed movement. A man came into view. A doctor? ... No. *Murari Pariyar.*

For a few seconds she was literally paralyzed by fear. She couldn't concentrate properly, her mind was whoozy. She fought to understand what was happening to her. Was she dreaming? Was it a nightmare? One minute she had been on a train on the journey to the rest of her life, the next she was here – with this strange man – admittedly a friend of her employers – looming over her. But where were they? She glanced around the room but they were nowhere to be seen.

Radhika tried to speak but nothing came out. Her mouth felt dry and parched, her tongue numb. She swallowed desperately and forcing the words through her cracked lips whispered, 'Where am I?' Then in increasing panic, 'Why am I here?'

Pariyar immediately tried to calm her. He told her that she had fainted on the train. Her employers had been forced to rush her to the hospital, where they had discovered germs in her blood. When pressed, he wouldn't say what kind of 'germs' they were. This immediately made her suspicious.

'I may be uneducated but I could tell by his eyes he was lying,' Radhika recalls. 'But I almost felt too weak to breathe, let alone argue with him.'

She subsided onto her bed, finding even the effort of her brief interaction with Pariyar exhausting. She tried to focus on regaining her strength instead.

It was only later when Radhika attempted to leave her bed for the first time to use the toilet that the full horror of what had happened to her finally struck home.

She was very weak and had been experiencing shooting pains in the region of her lower left abdomen for some time. Reaching beneath her brown hospital gown, Radhika's fingers encountering rough fabric. She pulled up the gown and peered down at the bandage that had been revealed. Even touching it tentatively hurt her. But what had happened? In a blinding flash of clarity, she realized that she must have undergone some kind of operation. But why that would have happened if she had some germs in her blood was beyond her comprehension.

'I felt so weak, but I summoned the courage to plead with Pariyar and the doctor to tell me the truth. They simply told me to return to my bed and calm down,' she recalls.

Over the next two months, Radhika was to be confined to the same bed in the hospital which, she later learned from her persistent questioning, was located in Chennai (Madras) in south-east India.

She was now 1,700km (1,056 miles) from her home and family. And no one she cared about knew where she was.

Radhika was not used to deceit. She came from a background and community in which the people were honest and simple and pretty much all shared common aims and attitudes towards life. Her current experiences were outside of anything she could have possibly imagined and, as such, it was some time before she was able to piece together the chain of events that had brought her to the hospital bed in Chennai.

'I stayed in hospital for two months without a single visitor except for Pariyar, who would [go] back and forth bringing me food.'

Confused, Radhika continued to beg the doctor and nurses to tell her what had happened to her. It was difficult as none of them spoke Nepali and Radhika spoke no Tamil. They tried to communicate with her in a mixture of Hindi and English, neither of which Radhika understood. This, of course, made it much easier for the doctor, in particular, to often shrug his shoulders and pretend that he didn't understand what the young woman was asking.

Radhika's movement was also restricted. She was taken for walks by the nurses but she wasn't allowed to move freely around the hospital. Alone and afraid, all she could do was wait. Control of her life had been taken away from her. She was a virtual prisoner and it soon became obvious that Pariyar was her jailer.

Matters came to a head one November morning. She woke to feel the warm winter sun beaming in through the window on to her face. The doctor began his rounds by asking Radhika to prepare herself for having her bandages removed.

Without as much as a reassuring touch or glance, he peeled back the bulky strips of gauze and revealed the skin beneath. Radhika stared in shock at the raw scar now snaking its way around the left side of her abdomen and waist like a ravenous python. It was about 12 inches (30.4cm) in length and the stitches were red and angry.

She couldn't fully comprehend what had happened to her yet. Or why. That was yet to come.

The frail 'mother' of the household, the woman who had greeted Radhika so warmly in Kathmandu was no longer so weak, it seemed.

It was true she had been ill, but she was now restored to health, thanks mainly to Radhika, who had certainly been needed by the family, just not in the role of housekeeper. Her use was of a much different, far more sinister kind. Young, healthy and alone, Radhika had been the perfect candidate for the job – the donor of a healthy kidney to a dying and desperate woman. The only thing was that no one had asked for her consent.

Radhika, it seemed, had paid the ultimate price for ticking all the right boxes in the family's search for the right candiate. The new set of clothes, toiletries and kindness that she had so gratefully accepted and which had led her to worry about how she could possibly pay back the family's generosity, had all been part of a calculated 'sweetener' to lure Radhika into the family's clutches.

And Sanjay Lama, far from being her friend, had been recruited by the family to find a suitable 'donor' for the mother. Murari Pariyar had been employed to make sure that the operation went smoothly. And it had – without a doubt. While Radhika slept her drug-induced sleep, her kidney was removed from her body and given to her wealthy employer, who was waiting in an adjacent operating theatre.

'I felt very, very sad,' she recalls. '[M]y life was spoiled.'

But her ordeal wasn't over yet.

Radhika's organ snatchers were keeping a careful eye on their 'investment'. They couldn't allow the girl to just walk out of the hospital and into a police station. Penalties for human trafficking and kidnapping, when they are taken seriously, are often harsh with long prison sentences, even in India and Nepal.

Besides which there was too much at stake, millions of dollars worth of trade and there was more money to be made out of an attractive young girl.

Unthinkably, although she wasn't to know it at the time, Radhika's nightmare was only just beginning.

Radhika gazed out of the window trying to absorb the hustle and bustle of this teeming new city, so very different from her native village or even Kathmandu. She had little idea where she was, only that Pariyar had taken her to a flat in Chennai after she was discharged from hospital.

Located on the Coromandel Coast of the Bay of Bengal, Chennai city has a population of 4.34 million and the wider area of metropolitan Chennai has an estimated population of over 8.2 million.

The city itself was established in the 17th century by the British, but some parts like Triplicane and its outskirts are almost 2,000 years old. Upon settling, the British developed Chennai into a major urban centre and naval base. By the 20th century, it had become an important administrative centre. Today, the city is an economic force to be reckoned with inside India. Its economy has a broad industrial base in the car, technology and hardware industries and it is also a major centre for music, art and culture in India. The city is also known for its classical dance shows and historic Hindu temples. The Tamil film industry, one of the largest in India, is based in the city; the soundtracks of the films it produces dominate its music scene.

Pariyar arranged for Radhika to be transported to a temporary apartment in central Chennai, which was being rented by Radhika's former employers.

While the patient had already jetted home to Kathmandu to recuperate in the luxurious surroundings of her townhouse, Radhika was left to recover from her ordeal in a much more pedestrian locale. On the second floor of a three-storey building in a small complex off a main road, the apartment was basic but clean and consisted of two bedrooms, a small lounge area and bathroom.

For Radhika it became hell. Some mornings when she awoke on the low wooden bed to the blankness of the white-washed walls, she would momentarily think she was back on the hospital ward. That thought immediately caused her to break out in a cold, clammy sweat.

In the end it was several days after her discharge from hospital that Radhika finally learned what had happened to her. Responding to a knock at the door Radhika opened it to find a young, very pale man standing there. He didn't look well and was visibly shaking. He just stared at Radhika. After a few moments she placed him – it was Sanjay, the youngest son of her former employers.

She felt the first stirrings of alarm. What now? While Sanjay had travelled from Kathmandu to Chennai with Radhika and the rest of his family at the beginning of the 'holiday', after that he had, to all intents and purposes, vanished – now, here he was on her doorstep.

When Radhika had originally met him, she had thought him very attractive. In his early 20s, Sanjay possessed the good looks of a Bollywood film star. With his thick mop of shiny black hair, he drew approving glances from most of the women who crossed his path. Before, Radhika could understand why – now all she could wonder was why he was here at the flat. It was quite obvious from the look on his face that he wasn't here to exchange pleasantries. She waited.

'He came to the apartment to confirm to me that I had been operated on for my kidney. It was by now of course very obvious what had happened but no one in the hospital had actually uttered the words to me. The doctor continued to be very furtive and evasive and no matter how many times I asked him the direct question, he wouldn't give me a direct answer. Now Sanjay had been sent by his family to set the record straight. I've no idea why they chose him – perhaps because he was the youngest – but it can't have been an easy thing to do.

'He greeted me formally by pressing his hands together and enquired briefly after my health before asking if he could come into the apartment. I led him in and he sat down awkwardly on a formal, wooden chair in the lounge. He was wearing a blue checked cotton shirt and modern, baggy jeans and I noticed that he was sweating profusely both on his forehead and under his arms where big wet patches had formed.'

Sanjay said that there was no easy way to say it other than that Radhika had been operated on for her kidney in order to save his mother's life. He paused and the silence seemed to stretch on forever.

'In that moment, I couldn't feel sad or even angry. I just felt numb. I think he sensed my shock, [my] sadness and shifted awkwardly in the chair. I looked directly at him ... stared straight into his eyes, searching for some clue to his true feelings.

'Tears were pricking them and I knew then that he felt some remorse for what his family had put me through.'

Sensing that he had let his guard down, Sanjay was keen to complete his mission as quickly as possible. Standing, he abruptly thrust a wad of notes into Radhika's hands, saying: 'This is your payment.'

A Terrible Awakening

It was 175,000 NPR (about £1,578).

Sanjay continued, 'You saved my mother's life'. Then he left the flat as abruptly as he had turned up.

Radhika says: 'I knew then for sure that this family had stolen a piece of my body. But what people couldn't see on the outside was that they had also taken a piece of my soul.'

How had her life come to this?, she thought as she tried to comprehend what had happened to her.

All her dreams of a new, bright future were lying ruined at her feet. She wanted to fling open the door and run out onto the street and find a way back home to her family, but the operation had taken its toll on her body and she still felt very ill and weak.

To remove her kidney, the doctor had made an incision around 12 inches (30.4cm) long before removing muscle, fat, and tissue. The tube that carries urine from the kidney to the bladder (ureter) and blood vessels was also cut away from the kidney before it was removed, along with Radhika's adrenal gland and some of her lymph nodes. Now she was left with only a bed to sleep on and no proper nursing care: Radhika had never felt so alone.

Once a daughter living in the bosom of a traditional and loving Nepalese family, she had always felt cherished by her parents and siblings, even though her brother's death had left a terrible void in her life that had been hard to fill. But after leaving home to help her family pay off a debt incurred by paying her sister's dowry, Radhika had wanted to prove she was independent. She had not kept in regular contact with them since arriving in Kathmandu.

How could she return to her village and tell her parents this terrible story? How could she reveal to them how gullible she had been? What would they think of her?

She just felt too ashamed to admit what had happened to her. Now, at the age of 16, her life was over.

Back in Kathmandu, Ramprasad and Maiya Phuyal were beside themselves with worry. While working at the vegetable market, their daughter had initially made monthly visits home but over the year, they had come to a halt. Radhika had made a vague reference to the new job she had been offered as a housekeeper somewhere in the city, but she had never confirmed if it had actually come to anything and her family remained none the wiser.

Seriously alarmed by Radhika's disappearance, they reported it to the city police, but the response was apathetic, to say the least. Kathmandu is a large place with over one million inhabitants and it's easy for people to disappear if they want to – or, more importantly, for people to make young, attractive women disappear, if *they* want to. But Ramprasad and Maiya didn't want to think about that scenario.

Radhika's entire family began a painstaking search of Kathmandu's streets for her, always refusing to believe that the worst could have happened and that she might be dead. Instead, they began to take solace in the notion that Radhika had left the country to pursue her dreams, as she had always wanted to. The alternative was simply unbearable.

A new life

FINALLY, Radhika was deemed fit enough to make the gruelling 1,700km (1,056 miles) train journey from Chennai in South India back home to Nepal.

As she gazed out of the carriage window, the events of the past three months flashed by. She felt foolish and naive as she recalled the excitement with which she had viewed the prospect of a holiday in India and the start of what she thought would be her brand new, better life.

A debilitating depression threatened to overwhelm her completely. She found it too difficult to shake off and it made it impossible for her to think clearly. It was made worse – if that were possible – by the presence of her travelling companion, Murari Pariyar.

The thought that she had to spend the next 40 hours in that man's company was almost more than Radhika could bear. He had done nothing but lie or mislead her from their very first meeting and she both feared and despised him. But Pariyar was now her shadow – literally *everywhere* Radhika went, the man invariably followed.

Lost in thought, Radhika recalled the painful events of the last few months. So much had changed, so much had altered in her life since Pariyar had first been introduced to her as a friend of her new employers. After the operation, it had quickly become apparent that he was much more than that. His job was to make sure that once she had 'donated' her kidney, she didn't speak of it to anyone else. She was a living testament to the operation that Pariyar and his friends had arranged and it was imperative that Radhika, like others before her, remained silent about what had happened to her.

She tried to dismiss Pariyar from her thoughts. The most important thing was that she was going home and she had to focus on that. But no matter how hard she tried, Pariyar was ever present. He was a difficult man to ignore. And the irritating squeak of his cheap plastic fashion shoes was a constant reminder of his presence. It was almost as if he wore them just for that purpose.

Forcing her weary eyes closed, Radhika shut Pariyar out of her vision at least, and pretended to sleep.

Pariyar studied the sleeping girl opposite him closely. She looked tired and wan. Despite her youth and obvious health, the operation, the loss of one kidney, had taken its toll on her. She was almost unrecognizable from the girl he had first met in Nepal.

It didn't matter though. Radhika had done what he needed of her and anyway, he had further plans for the girl. There was really only one way to make sure she kept her mouth shut – one tried and already tested method which had, in the past, kept other girls on side. He knew it would work with Radhika. Smiling, Pariyar recalled the 'Quote of the Day' that he had read in a Nepalese newspaper ages ago, but had taken to heart – *'Keep your friends close and your enemies closer'*. They had a particular resonance now. After being tricked into losing a kidney, Radhika wasn't feeling particularly well disposed towards him. She was concentrating on the negatives of her situation, rather than the positives of her kidney 'donation', of which there were arguably many, he mused.

Radhika was, after all, young enough to recover from this business. She was healthy enough to survive with one kidney and, more importantly, she was about to be rich by her own standards, and those of her peers, as the recipient's family would pay her directly for her service to them. From experience he knew that girls such as Radhika usually commanded about 175,000 NPR (about £1,578) for a kidney from grateful family members.

In many ways she should thank him for what he'd done. That little operation had saved her from abject poverty. The fact that in most cases the girls involved didn't get to keep the money was another matter altogether and one he carefully ignored.

Pariyar examined Radhika. She was a very pretty girl, even in this exhausted state, recovering from a rigorous operation. It was obvious she was a very good investment for them.

Yes, he thought smiling, he had plans for little Radhika.... Ones that would help keep her mouth shut and also be profitable. Once they got back to Kathmandu, marriage to a member of the organization – one of his own cousins – would help keep her in line. And the money she was about to receive would more than pay her 'dowry'. He was doing her another service. Marriage, after all, was every Nepalese girl's dream. And he was helping broker the deal. He smirked. All considered, Radhika Phuyal should be very grateful to him. He had changed her life beyond recognition, after all.

After the long hours of travel, Radhika awoke to find the train rocking to a halt. She was completely disorientated and before she could even blink, Pariyar had gathered together her meagre possessions and had ushered her off the train. They were immediately swallowed up by the station crowd and the sounds and smells found at any railway station in South Asia. The bright colours of the women's saris and kurtas, the overpowering reek of fried food and overly ripe fruit, mixed together with the strong smell of sewage and the almost painful sounds of the screech of brakes and the piercing whistle of the trains all merged together in Radhika's tired and over-taxed mind.

She was dimly aware of Pariyar shepherding her through the crowds, aware of his hand gripping her elbow tightly, aware of him guiding her past obstacles, almost protectively, as if they were man and wife rather than kidnapper and victim. She was aware of him speaking to someone and money exchanging hands as the snippets of conversation in languages that she simply didn't understand drifted in and out of her consciousness.

Like a puppet being directed by its master, Radhika allowed herself to be pushed and pulled by Pariyar, following him through the people and traffic until she finally took the last few steps onto the vehicle looming in front of her that would take her on the last leg to Kathmandu.

A New Life

Sinking onto the dirty, torn seat of the dilapidated jeep, Radhika pressed her weary head against the window pane and tried to take in the enormity of what had happened to her over the past three months. Just 16, she had endured more horror than fate deals most people in a lifetime. She spent the rest of the journey drifting along in a strange soporific state, for the most part unaware of the changing landscape as the vehicle pushed on across the border, leaving India far behind.

Finally, when Nepal's breathtaking patchwork of brightly coloured temples and lush green hills came into view, Radhika jerked into awareness of her surroundings, but the searing pain in the side of her body quickly overcame the sheer pleasure of her homecoming. She had, for a moment, forgotten the circumstances that had brought her to be riding this bus from India to Nepal.

Nearing the city, Radhika should have been full of joy at the prospect of being reunited with her close-knit family. She knew they would most probably be sick with worry by now after her prolonged absence. But how could she look them in the eye and admit that she had been so stupid? What would her aged grandmother think of her?

Without a doubt, she had shamed her family and perhaps it was for the best that they should think of her as being dead. In the short term, Radhika needed time and space to regain more strength and clear her mind. At least being back in the familiar surroundings of her home city would help her to do that – or so she hoped.

With that in mind, when the bus finally arrived at its final destination, Radhika once more allowed her puppet master to take control and followed him where he led.

This time it was to the surprising location of a flat owned by his mother-in-law. The apartment was a far cry from the one in Chennai, where she had been taken to recuperate by Pariyar. A top-floor flat in a modest apartment block near the centre of Kathmandu, the furnishings were sparse and it was in need of a good clean. A ragged pair of red curtains, hung in the main living room, were the only attempt to make the place more homely.

At first Radhika was still so weak and mentally exhausted that she wasn't really aware of her surroundings and certainly wasn't strong enough to ask Pariyar why he had bought her here. When she eventually started to feel slightly more herself, she spent her days worrying about how she could approach her family again. How could she even begin to tell them what had happened to her? They were loving and simple people. A world in which men drugged young girls and took their kidneys without their consent was simply beyond their comprehension. It was frankly beyond hers, so how could they possibly understand?

She was wracked with guilt and shame.

How could she have been so stupid?

A few days after she arrived at the apartment, Radhika was introduced by the Pariyars to a man called Rajesh Kumar. He was fair-skinned and had long dark hair. He was, Radhika thought, quite handsome. Even so, she was still very shocked when Pariyar's mother-in-law asked Radhika to marry him.

'I was completely taken aback. And, of course, [I] said "no", but it was made clear to me that I had no choice ... [T]he rituals of marriage were forced upon me.'

A New Life

A big Bollywood fan, Radhika had occasionally picked up old magazines and newspapers at the Balaju market, where she used to work selling vegetables. She spent hours poring over the glossy images showing beautiful people who invariably had love marriages that changed their lives for the better. In these fairy-tale plots, the protagonists had the freedom to fall head-over-heels in love first and then marry the partners that they had chosen. In the end they got their dream ending. Radhika had also believed that could happen to her, that she would meet and fall in love and live happily ever after. She knew that it was possible. She had seen it with her own eyes … admittedly on the pages of a magazine.

Radhika's reality was far different, however. She recalls, 'Pariyar's mother-in-law threw a red sari at me and barked at me to put it on.

'Then Rajesh, my husband-to-be, roughly stained a red *sindur** onto my forehead. [He was] in a temper and slung red beads and bangles at me.

'A Hindu priest was called to the house and I was forced to go through with the rituals of marriage.'

Marriage in the Hindu religion is solemnized in accordance with scriptures that date back several thousand years. It is the bonding of two souls (man and woman) and also the merging of two families and, as such, is taken very seriously. The ceremony itself is usually extremely intricate and detailed, involving many different stages, each of which is symbolic and has its origin in ancient times.

A Hindu marriage usually takes place over several days. The practices include the ritual cleansing of the bride and groom in their homes, while a priest chants 'mantras' from

*A vermilion powder smeared onto the forehead and hairline usually of married women, but also as part of the marriage ritual.

the Vedas, the ancient Hindu scriptures. Certain elements are used in the various ceremonies to represent matters important to the union such as fresh flowers (beauty); coconut (fertility); rice (signifying the food necessary to sustain life); ghee or purified butter (used to feed the sacred fire); and kumkum or vermilion (good luck).

As her own marriage began with *Ganesh Sthapana**, once more, Radhika's mind drifted to the Bollywood heroines who had influenced how she had wanted her own ideal marriage to be. In her dreams, Radhika stood dressed in a beautiful, beaded creation by Indian fashion designer Tarun Tahiliani, her hair beautifully groomed and her hands, arms, legs and feet intricately decorated with beautiful henna patterns. The reality was about as different from this as it could possibly be. Instead, Radhika felt ashamed and dirty, dressed as she was in the shabby, threadbare red sari that Pariyar's mother-in-law had probably worn to buy food from the local market. Only the *tilhari*, the gold cylindrical pendant woven into red beads, which Rajesh had thrown at her in such a temper but which she now wore around her neck, added a hint of glamour to the proceedings.

The ceremony continued with *Grah Shanti* (a prayer to the nine planets of the solar system) and *Kanyadaan* ('giving away the girl'), usually one of the most emotional of the Hindu marriage ceremony as it is when the father of the bride (or an elderly relative in his absence) entrusts his daughter to the groom, thus signifying parental consent. The bride's right hand is placed on the groom's right hand. Sacred verses are chanted and the couple exchange garlands. The groom holds the hand of the bride and takes vows to

---

* *A prayer invoking Lord Ganesh, whose divine grace dispels all evils and is meant to ensure the smooth running of the ceremony and bring happiness and prosperity.*

love her and protect her throughout his life. In this instance, however, the issue of parental consent was overlooked completely. Radhika's parents had no idea that the marriage was taking place in the first place. In fact, they weren't even sure if their beloved daughter was alive so how could they give their consent to this marriage?

Radhika was heartbroken. On top of everything else she had suffered, she was now being forced to marry a man who she'd only just met, without her family present, in less than salubrious surroundings. She wondered how things could possibly get any worse.

Radhika still had to endure several more rituals, ones that in other circumstances she would have felt happy to undertake but in this instance were just dreadful. She watched as the priest performed *Granthi Bandhan*, in which he tied a wedding knot symbolizing the permanent union between the couple as husband and wife and also the union of two individuals into one entity; *Agni Puja*, in which a fire is lit in the middle of the mandap to symbolize the illumination of mind, knowledge and happiness; the remainder of the ceremony is conducted around this fire; and like a robot she forced herself to perform her duties in *Shilarohana*, during which the bride places her right foot on a stone and the bridegroom directs her to be as firm as the stone in his house so that they can face their difficulties together.

Difficulties.... Radhika couldn't help thinking how enormous the *difficulties* ahead were going to be. Parental consent and approval were essential to a proper and successful marriage in Nepalese culture. How could such forced and rushed nuptials bring them anything but bad luck?

* Agni is the god of fire and messenger of the gods as well as being the acceptor of sacrifice..

The priest seemed oblivious to Radhika's distress. She wondered what stories he might have been told by her captors to allow him to conduct this marriage in good conscience. Perhaps he had been told that her parents were dead or were too ill to attend the wedding? Perhaps he just didn't care? Perhaps he had received a hefty donation to help speed things along? Whatever the truth was, Radhika felt that she had no choice other than to passively comply with his orders in between mantras.

The ceremony continued with *Laja Homah* in which the bride offers puffed rice and prayers to the sacred fire, praying to Yama, the god of death to grant the groom long life, health, happiness and prosperity. During *Mangal Fera,* Radhika followed her new husband around the sacred fire four times to signify the goals of *dharma* ('righteousness'), *artha* ('financial success'), *kama* ('energy and passion') and *moksha* ('liberation'); and in *Saptapadi* she and her groom took seven steps around the flames to reflect Hindu philosophy, which states that if two people walk seven steps they will remain lifelong friends.

Then the rituals became more intimate and even more upsetting and uncomfortable for Radhika, as a result. During *Saubhagya Chinha*, Rajesh blessed Radhika by putting *sindur* on her forehead and in *Haridaya-Sparsha,* the bride and bridegroom touched each other's hearts. Radhika felt ashamed and somehow unholy. The marriage was a sham. She wasn't even sure if it would be legal in the underhand way it was being carried out. But who would believe her? And what could she do anyway? She would be ruined in the eyes of her family and society as a whole.

Finally, they performed *Chathurthi Karma* in which the bride and groom feed each other four times to nourish the bone, muscle, skin and soul, before *Aashirvaad* (blessings) brought the excruciating ceremony to a close.

For most Hindu brides, the wedding ceremony is the culmination of a life's preparation for that moment and is, therefore, something to look forward to and to be cherished. For Radhika, still aged just 16, it represented yet another event over which she had no control.

What should have been one of the happiest moments of her life instead made her feel empty inside and emphasized her utter isolation. Her family had not been present at her wedding. Worse still, they didn't even know where she was. Her sister, Parvati, lived in Kathmandu, for all Radhika knew not that far from where she was staying, yet she had no means of contacting her. She was lost.

'I slept alone that night. I couldn't bear to feel my husband's skin next to mine. I felt so sad, I cried myself to sleep,' Radhika recalls.

Rajesh, her new husband, sat up alone drinking himself into a stupor, imbibing a disgusting concoction of home-brewed alcohol.

The only thing Radhika could call her own was the vast bundle of dirty Nepalese notes that she had been given in exchange for her kidney. But it wasn't long before Rajesh made his demands, extracting 55,000 NPR (around £495). Radhika kept the remainder of the money in a black handbag, which she carried around with her everywhere, even sleeping with it at night. This was her way out and she knew she had to keep hold of it, whatever else happened.

This money was her only possession and she knew that she would need it to buy her freedom.

'Looking back, I think my husband and his associates allowed me to hang onto [some of] it to keep me sweet. They believed it would make me feel as though I had some control over the situation, although I didn't, of course.... Anyway, Rajesh knew he could access the money anytime he wanted. If I refused, he would beat me.'

Later, Rajesh demanded another 100,000 NPR (around £900) as dowry, which she was forced to give him. Finally, he ordered Radhika to hand over the rest of her stash for 'safekeeping'. She had nothing left to call her own or to fall back on if she needed money urgently. She was now totally dependent on her husband.

In the 'honeymoon period' of their marriage, Rajesh appeared to be mild-mannered and even quite caring at times. He made an effort to be a considerate lover when their marriage was finally consummated about three weeks after the ceremony took place. But there was a darker reason for his behaviour.

'I know now that he was brainwashing me into thinking … he really loved me,' Radhika says. 'It was just another part of the grooming process – breaking down my defences still further; preparing me for what was to come.'

Rajesh wasted no time in moving his new wife away from the small room in the flat they had been sharing in Kathmandu with Pariyar's mother-in-law. While this could be read as an eager groom wanting to set up home with his new bride in a place of their own, the truth was that the longer Radhika remained in Kathmandu, the greater the risk that Radhika's family might discover her. So they travelled to Rajesh's home district of Sindhupalchowk, 20km (12.4 miles) north-east of the Kathmandu Valley.

The area is a tourist destination. People come to watch the Melamchi River flowing placidly through this poor hill area and in the village of Palchowk (which provides the second half of the district's name) stands the 100-year-old temple of Shri Jai Bageshwari Devi. On Saturdays, locals arrive to perform the elaborate Hindu rite of *Pancha Bali* during which buffalo sacrifices are made, commanding up to 10,000 NPR (around £90) each. A discerning person might ask where the money comes from – the province is poor, after all. In fact, the area's wealth comes from a sinister source of trade: it is the predominant exporter of young girls to brothels in India – and this lucrative business has made many of the locals extraordinarily wealthy.

But Radhika wasn't aware of this when she moved into her new marital home, a single-storey red, mud house that lacked electricity or running water. Although this was not unusual in the village, it was obvious that the house was rundown and Radhika sensed that her husband's family was not as well established as others in the village. But calling on her natural optimism, Radhika chose to make the best of her life. This was her lot now.

She soon developed a daily routine, cutting the grass, sowing grains, gathering wood and collecting water from the local well. Soon after moving into their new home, Radhika realized that she had other things to concern herself with. She discovered that she was pregnant and immediately felt an intense and unwavering love for her unborn child. Suddenly she had someone other than herself to worry about, to fight for, someone to call her own.

But Radhika's pregnancy became the catalyst for a terrible onset of calculated abuse by her husband. Rajesh had already revealed his true colours, getting drunk on a home brew of alcohol and wheat grain and soon he was keeping his wife subdued with a daily dose of violence. He would shout and scream at Radhika for no reason, railing at her as he worked himself up into such a rage that he ended up using her as his personal punching bag, splitting her lips and sometimes throttling her until she could barely breathe. This only worsened when she fell pregnant. Rajesh didn't seem to care about the safety of his unborn child.

It was a miracle that she did not lose her baby, but somehow he – she thought of her baby already as a 'he' – survived, hanging onto life. She took comfort from the fact he was a fighter and she vowed that whatever it took, whatever she had to put up with she would always love her child. She would protect him no matter what came her way. She just had to work out how to do so. But after 10 months of marriage, matters were taken out of her hands. She awoke one morning, after a brutal disagreement with Rajesh, to find that he had fled their home. He was gone.

Initially, Radhika was overcome with feelings of intense relief. No more beatings. No more putting up with a man who abused her, both physically and mentally. No more worrying about the safety of her baby. Then reality sunk in. She was destitute: her husband had made off with all her money. After a few panicked minutes, she made herself calm down. She had someone other than herself to fight for now, after all. They would survive.

Placing her hand on her stomach, she whispered to her unborn child, 'It's just you and me now, my precious. *Together, forever.*'

A bright star is born

ROHAN* set himself apart as a survivor from the moment he entered the world at 11.30 p.m. on 30 March 2004.

Radhika was bent over sowing grains when the first labour pains began to erupt in her pregnant belly. She felt a mixture of excitement and fear as she calmly walked the kilometre across the ruggedly ploughed fields to alert her mother-in-law, Seti, to her child's imminent arrival.

When Radhika first met Rajesh's mother, her immediate impression was that she had once been quite beautiful. In her late 30s, she was small in stature and frail in build. She carried herself with grace and took pride in sweeping back her long black hair into a neat bun each morning, taking care to hide the grey strands. Seti never spoke of her husband, except to say that he had passed away some years previously. Radhika sensed though – more through what Seti didn't say – that life had been hard for her even when her husband was alive. Perhaps he possessed some of the same harsh personality traits that Rajesh displayed.

Seti lived in a small, two-storey mud house close to Radhika's marital home. In keeping with many houses in the

*Radhika named her son Roshan ('bright star' in Nepali). His name was later changed to the more Hindi-sounding 'Rohan' by brothel workers in India.

village, it was covered with cow dung and surrounded by a small lawn. Inside, Seti shared her home with a buffalo and two goats and the upstairs was used for storing hay.

While Seti was certainly no replacement for Radhika's own wonderful mother, Maiya, whom Radhika still missed with all her heart, she was extremely fond of the woman and believed the feeling was returned. Radhika was also grateful to her; just the presence of an older woman, moreover someone she felt understood some of what she was going through somehow made life more bearable.

Radhika and Seti often spent time together working the land adjoining their neighbouring homes. They grew vegetables such as peas, pumpkins and spinach. The crop enabled them to be self-sufficient and any left over produce could be sold to bring in much-needed additional income. The pair also performed household chores together. Despite this, Radhika never confided in Seti about Rajesh. Even though Seti appeared to be aware of her son's failings and would often berate him for his laziness and ungentlemanly behaviour towards his wife, Radhika wanted to protect her from the full horror of her son's cruelty.

Following Rajesh's disappearance, Radhika found it strange that Seti hadn't really commented on it. To all intents and purposes she didn't appear to find it that odd that her son had up and left, abandoning his pregnant wife and child. Even so, Radhika had felt obliged to tell the woman something, so she informed her that there had been a heated argument. As she watched Seti digest this, Radhika suspected that she was well aware of her son's volatile nature and that he had perhaps displayed similar violence in the past. After that, Radhika sometimes glimpsed a strange look in Seti's eyes when they rested on her. After a while, she realized that it was shame – that somehow Seti felt that Rajesh's behaviour was her own responsibility. This wasn't the case: while Seti, perhaps unwittingly, had contributed to her son's spoiled and petulant temperament, Rajesh was now a grown man and Radhika felt strongly that he was accountable for his own actions. Anyway, over time she had begun to love Seti and she wanted to shield the older woman from further pain.

When Radhika appeared at her house on the morning of Rohan's birth, Seti immediately gathered together some of the other women from the village to help her daughter-in-law through her first birth.

Radhika's labour was long, drawn-out and difficult, not just because she was so weak from malnutrition – on some days she could barely afford to eat one meal, although Seti helped out wherever she could – but also because the beatings that Rajesh had given her had taken their toll on her already beleaguered body. Plus, she only had one kidney to rely on now. In mind-numbing pain, Radhika was in labour from 5 a.m. until 11.30 p.m., but she didn't care.

'All I could think about was seeing the child I had longed for so desperately – someone who I could love and someone who would love me unconditionally and unquestionably in return.'

When her baby finally made his appearance in the world, even that wasn't without trauma. 'As the baby's head began to emerge I could see that the umbilical chord was wrapped around its neck. It wasn't moving or even crying. Seti immediately grabbed a knife and cut the chord with a sharp blade. Then she slapped my child on the bottom and suddenly it came to life. That's when my beautiful baby boy cried for the first time. The sound was like nothing else I had [ever] heard.

'He was adorable and healthy. I vowed then that this was a part of me [that] no one would ever take away.'

Radhika proudly named her son 'Roshan'* and focused her attentions on keeping her son well and happy. For the first time Radhika was truly contented. She was living peacefully in her home with her new son and Seti, who moved in with Radhika shortly after Rohan's birth. Survival was still a tough business but somehow they managed to grow enough food to live on. More than that Radhika now had something to live for. Thoughts of Rajesh and his brutal treatment were superseded by the awe-inspiring being who was her son. He made her more determined to succeed; he gave her hope when previously there had been little or none.

But her baby's existence also forced Radhika to face facts. She couldn't be stupid or naive any more. She had to protect Rohan. She made up her mind that if Rajesh returned, she would take their child and leave – most probably for Kathmandu, where she could set up another vegetable stall at Balaju market. She was just 17 and life wasn't over for her yet: she had proved she was a survivor and she would make sure her son would be one, too.

Back in Kathmandu, Radhika's older sister, Parvati, was thinking of Radhika and wondering what could have happened to her. Several years had passed since she had last seen her little sister and her mind strayed to her, as it often did. It was all so strange. Of all of the Phuyal children, Radhika seemed the least likely to take risks. She was a

*To avoid confusion, I refer to him as Rohan everywhere else in the book.

dreamer admittedly but she wouldn't deliberately hurt their parents, their grandmother, by cutting herself off so ruthlessly. Something must have happened to her. But what?

Radhika had always been a shy and sensitive child and she had been quiet and accepting as a young woman. But perhaps that was the problem?, Parvati mused. Had she been *too* accepting? In which case anything could have happened to her.

When Radhika had turned up in the city, earning her living at Balaju market, at least her family had known where she was. As time passed, even though she continued to send money back home, Radhika's contact with them had become less frequent. Now, years had lapsed since anyone had heard from her and everyone was still beside themselves with worry. She felt her parents' hope everytime she saw them, hope that perhaps she had heard something about her younger sister. Then Parvati shared their pain when they realized that she had nothing new to tell them.

Initially, the Phuyals had searched for Radhika in the city. They reported her disappearance to the police, but nothing had been done. In the grand scheme of things, Radhika was just one of the many young girls who vanished into the darkness of Kathmandu's streets so why should the police take it seriously?

Parvati, who was more than a beautiful face, also possessing a keen intelligence and determination, just wouldn't, *couldn't* accept that was it. That her sister's life could mean so little; that these men could treat her as if she didn't exist. So, she began to ask her own questions around the city about Radhika. While they hadn't been close as children, mainly due to their age difference, as the eldest sibling in the family Parvati believed that it was her duty to do everything to find Radhika that she possibly could. So she persevered. She realized later that all the time she searched, she had subconsciously been imagining the worst when she received a phone call one morning at her apartment in Dallu, a smart residential district in West Kathmandu, informing her otherwise.

When she picked up the phone, Parvati heard a strange male voice greet her with the traditional 'namaste'. He then introduced himself as 'Rajesh Kumar', her new brother-in-law. Stunned, Parvati listened as Rajesh then broke the news that Radhika was pregnant. While Parvati reeled with shock, Rajesh carried on speaking, assuring her that she had nothing to worry about as he was from a 'good family', something he kept emphasizing, obviously aware that was important to a high-caste Brahmin family such as the Phuyals.

But even as he reassured Parvati that his background was suitable, she was aware of a growing feeling that something was wrong with Rajesh. That there was something in the tone of his voice that she didn't quite like. There and then, she promised herself that she would make the trip out to see her sister. She would see first-hand what kind of life her sister had made for herself. Parvati would make sure that Radhika was ok.

Parvati pushed the man for further detail but he prevaricated. He was cagey not just about his own whereabouts, but concerning any details to do with her sister's life and health. By the time the call ended, instead of feeling better, Parvati felt very uneasy and not a little upset. After careful thought she decided that until she found out more information, she would keep the conversation to herself. Her parents weren't particularly old, it was true, but neither were they young, and Radhika's disappearance had already caused them great distress. In the end it was several months before Parvati was able to take time away from her family's business commitments to make the journey to see Radhika. On reflection, she wished she had made the trip far earlier. By the time she reached Sindhupalchowk, it was more than three years since she had last seen Radhika.

After an arduous five-hour bus journey from Kathmandu to Sindhupalchowk, Parvati arrived at the village. She was greeted by a gaggle of local busybodies, who, after eliciting information from her about her journey, her family, her life, pointed her in the direction of Radhika's house.

During their conversation Parvati learned something that stunned her – some of the women told her that Radhika's kidney had been taken from her. They spoke about it in a very matter of fact manner, as if it was neither that strange nor that important. In fact, it had happened to one or two of the other girls in the village. At the time Parvati was shocked as she had never heard of such a thing happening before and it was beyond her comprehension that her little sister might have suffered such a horrible fate. She was later to discover that in certain parts of rural Nepal, it was not uncommon for several people in a village to have had their organs harvested – the monetary rewards were often the difference between life and death and the financial benefits lucrative enough to make even such a dangerous operation attractive.

When Parvati finally found Radhika, the young woman was pale and there was nothing for her or her baby to eat. She was so weak and malnourished that she couldn't even breastfeed her six-month-old child. Despite this, Parvati's first emotions at seeing her sister were those of elation.

'It was incredible to see her familiar beautiful features,' she recalls. 'She looked at me and her face broke into a shy but beaming smile. I think Radhika was unsure about how I would react ... and perhaps thought I would be angry [with her]. But how could I be?

'Here in front of me was the little sister I had written off as dead.... [W]e ran towards one another and embraced. As I held Radhika tightly, I could feel her breastbone and ribcage protruding through her skin. I knew from that moment that she had been through a terrible ordeal.

'We hail from a humble family but we have always been able to afford enough to eat. It was clear that Radhika could not. Of course the villagers had already alerted me to my sister's kidney ordeal but she did not [appear to want to] raise it and I didn't want to frighten her away again or make her feel uncomfortable.

'I decided to leave the issue at that point until she was ready to discuss it. Besides, there were more pressing things to deal with – like Radhika's terrible living conditions.'

Radhika was living in a hovel. After a little bit of time, she explained to Parvati that her husband had disappeared with the family savings, leaving her all but destitute.

Even years later as Parvati recalls that time, tears well up in her lovely brown eyes and roll slowly down her face.

'Her good-for-nothing husband had left her beaten down in every way and my sister was destitute. He had [tried to dupe] me into believing he was a responsible man – [but] nothing could have been further from the truth.'

Perhaps most shocking of all for Parvati was the discovery from one of the villagers that Rajesh had lied about his caste. He was not a descendant of the Brahmins, like his wife. In fact he hailed from the Shudra caste, a much lower caste than the Phuyals.

Parvati was horrified. The implications for her sister, even though she had been forced into an intercaste marriage, were still unthinkable. To elder, more traditional members of the Phuyal family such as their revered grandmother, Hari Prem, Radhika would be a virtual outcast. Even worse, Parvati's husband would now refuse to accommodate Radhika in the family home as Parvati had originally suggested.

In the end, all she could do was hand over the modest sum of 800 NPR (£7.15) that she had secretly saved for her sister before she left and pray for the best possible outcome.

Parvati says: 'I kissed my sister and Rohan goodbye, told them I loved them and pleaded with them to stay safe until my next visit. It was the last I saw of them for [many] years.'

Parvati's visit breathed new life into Radhika. Invigorated, she tried to make the best of her meagre surroundings with the money her sister had given her. For the sake of her baby son, who was her world, she would make things right.

She swept the mud floors of their humble house, laid new rush matting down that she had woven and made an effort to magic nutritious meals from the small vegetable patch adjacent to the house. Seti was doing her best to also help her daughter-in-law and grandson but her means were limited: she quite simply didn't have the strength or the financial backing to support the vulnerable mother and child. Radhika, in turn, felt awful that she couldn't help Seti more.

By the time Rohan was a year old, Radhika was showing the same signs of severe exhaustion that she had displayed during her sister's visit. Poor nutrition coupled with the impact of living with one kidney and the aftermath of a traumatic labour had left her feeling exceptionally drained and very weak. She was desperately in need of help and also was lonely.

One day two men, 28-year-old Krishna 'Purne' Pariyar, and 35-year-old Rajan Pariyar, turned up at the house, claiming to be her husband's cousins. She opened the door and saw two clean-cut, handsome and well-spoken men. During their subsequent conversation, she convinced herself that these men were made in the same mould as the ones with which she had grown up, that they were decent men, not like Murari Pariyar or her husband.

They explained that they had come to the village in search of work, but told Radhika that they had lost track of time. Finding themselves stranded in the village at night, they remembered that Rajesh and his wife lived there. The men knew that they had to pay them a call or appear discourteous. The men's explanation did strike Radhika as slightly odd, even though it was true that darkness was setting in. She quickly dismissed her misgivings. They were family after all, but even though she was living in a small village where it was common for people to show hospitality to weary visitors, she was aware of the proprieties and quickly made it clear that there was no room for the two men to sleep in her house. They agreed that they would find accommodation with other acquaintances in the village and promised to return in the morning.

They duly returned the next day and after further discussion expressed great concern at Radhika's situation.

After some consideration, they informed her that they would escort her to Parvati's house in Kathmandu. They couldn't in all conscience leave her here to fend for herself in such circumstances.

Radhika recalls, 'I was so excited I could hardly contain myself. Parvati hadn't seen Rohan for months and I desperately needed a hug and some reassurance from my sister, too. I was aware that there was an issue with me staying with my sister Parvati longterm. She would have been happy with the arrangement but her husband was unhappy with me marrying beneath our caste and had forbidden me entering the house. But I hoped that once I arrived on their doorstep with Rohan, he would warm to my little boy and change his mind.

'I wasted no time in gathering up the few belongings [that] Rohan and I owned and strapped him to my back with a scarf. We were leaving this hard life behind and heading to the city.

'I was happy for another reason. It was always my dream to make sure Rohan received the education I had been denied and being in Kathmandu would hopefully make that possible.'

And so Radhika and Rohan joined the Pariyars on their journey to Kathmandu. Once again she was putting her faith and trust in a couple of strangers. She spared little thought for the life she was leaving behind.

Radhika felt elated on the return journey to Kathmandu. She had always believed that the city would help her fulfil her dreams and while that hadn't happened last time, maybe, on this occasion, the gods would be with her. Her greatest wish was to send Rohan to a good school so even if Parvati turned them away, they would be in the best place possible to ensure her son a bright future. Or so she believed.

At the end of the two-hour bus journey from Sindhupalchowk to Kathmandu, however, the taxi hailed by Purne and Rajan did not head for Radhika's sister's neighbourhood, as they had promised. While Radhika had not been inside her sister's house, she knew roughly where it was and she had a good sense of the city and its various districts. Feeling helpless, she clutched Rohan to her, waiting for what would happen next. She didn't have a good feeling about it though.

Finally, the taxi drew to a halt outside a building – the Hong Kong Guest House. Radhika recognized where they were – the outlying Balaju region of the city, where she had sold vegetables in the market almost four years ago.

Instantly on her guard, Radhika started to feel a familiar sense of dread. With a great deal of assumed calm, she asked her companions why they had brought her to the hotel instead of to her sister's house, only to shrink back in her seat when the two men turned on her, barking almost in unison: 'We are in no hurry. *Shut up!*'

Purne left Radhika and Rohan in the company of Rajan, the man he claimed was his brother. Despite his earlier outburst, Rajan calmly reassured Radhika that they would reach her sister's house in due course. He then led Radhika and Rohan into the hotel, taking her into a room. Radhika watched him carefully as he flicked through the TV channels while swigging his beer.

For the first time since they had started their journey, Radhika began to feel real fear. How could she have left her home for this? Had she again been too trusting? She held

Rohan ever closer and whispered: 'We'll be just fine. I love you' in his tiny shell-like ear.

She pleaded with Rajan to take her to Parvati's home, but her cries fell on deaf ears. It was almost as if she and Rohan were invisible. Finally, after hours of being held a virtual prisoner, Radhika got the truth from him, the one that she had been dreading since her arrival in the guest house, when Rajan bellowed at her agressively, 'You are not going to your sister's place. You are coming with me!'

Once again Radhika was forced to pack her bags. Silently, praying for some miracle to happen, some hero to come and rescue them from this nightmare, she strapped baby Rohan onto her back with a pink, threadbare pashmina and stood back to let whatever was about to happen occur.

She didn't believe what Rajan had told her. Why should she? He had already lied to her twice. This time the promise of a holiday in a new and exotic land had been replaced by one of a job at a grocery store in Biratnagar, Nepal's second largest city located near the Indian border in the south-eastern region. She noticed that Rajan didn't even try to meet her eyes when he spoke to her.

This time Radhika didn't attempt to put up a fight. She had become attuned to obeying male authority and the implied threat of violence made her even more compliant. Now she had Rohan to take care of, to live for. On one level, she knew that the job offer was a lie, but on another she continued to hope that she was wrong, for Rohan's sake.

'I knew it would only take one wrong word to unleash the terrible temper that appeared to be bubbling [beneath] Rajan's hard-faced exterior. I didn't want Rohan to witness the sort of violence [that] he had been forced to endure from his father while [he was still] in my womb so I told myself to be strong and endure whatever the gods were about to unleash.'

And so, at 8 p.m. in March 2005, Radhika boarded yet another bus for yet another unknown destination, this time with her tiny son, her 'bright star', clutched firmly in her arms. Whatever happened next, Radhika swore that she would deal with it for Rohan's sake.

THE ROAD
TO
DHANDA

Welcome to Assam

IT was the familiar smell of citrus trees wafting in through the train windows that told Radhika that she was in India. It was little more then two years since she had first crossed the border from Nepal in the innocent belief that she was going on holiday and beginning a great adventure. Instead, she had become an unwitting pawn in the lucrative international trade in human organs and her kidney had been ripped out of her against her will.

It was almost unthinkable to Radhika that she could still be under the control of the trafficking 'mafia', but Purne and Rajan had claimed to be related to her husband, who had himself been introduced to her by Murari Pariyar, in the first place. With all this in mind, Radhika had little option but to conclude that this was the case. Had the gods really deserted her? Where was Lakshmi now? What had she done in her previous lives to deserve all this?

As Radhika watched the train steam on she felt at odds with the beautiful landscape outside. Cobalt blue skies contrasted breathtakingly against the endless green fields in which lucrative tea leaves grew. Occasionally, Radhika would catch a glimpse of the colourfully clad female harvesters, wending their way down the hills, delicately balancing reed baskets on their heads. They appeared so free and easy in their work.

Why couldn't she have found such a job? Was it really too much to ask for? She had always been prepared to work hard to improve her life, but for some reason no matter what she tried she always seemed to end up in trouble.

She did her best to stay calm throughout the journey for Rohan's sake, but unlike the last time she had travelled from Kathmandu to India, she now had bitter experience to draw on. In one sense, motherhood had made her feel stronger and she certainly had an overwhelming desire to shield Rohan from harm's way but in another sense she felt far more vulnerable. Now she had another person depending on her, someone so little that he couldn't fend for himself. Yet, she was now powerless and in the hands of Purne and Rajan Pariyar. She hadn't had any choice other than to go with them and had sensed that any objections that she might have would have been met with violence. She was not willing to risk her well being when Rohan's was at stake.

Taking a deep breath, she stared out of the train window and willed herself to stay positive, to stay calm.

After getting off the train, Radhika's route from Nepal to India was different to last time. She travelled with Rajan to India by bus, journeying from Kathmandu via Kakarvitta, on the Nepal–India border at the eastern end of Nepal's 922km (573 mile) long East–West Highway. It took 13 hours to make the gruelling 610km (379 mile) drive from the capital and Rohan, who was still so small, was hot and restless by the time they disembarked.

Looking at the sad and confused expression on his tiny face, Radhika could literally feel her heart breaking with sorrow. Surely she should be able to provide a better future for her child than this? She couldn't help thinking that if she had been allowed to stay at school and finish her education, as she'd so wished, she would be in a completely different position today. She would never have come across Lama, or any of the other men who had helped bring her to this. Now, her primary concern was how to keep her son, her one 'bright star' safe.

Rajan Pariyar clearly shared none of Radhika's concerns for Rohan. She already knew he wasn't kind and recognized that he could easily become violent, if provoked. That was something she wanted to avoid at all costs so, she said nothing, remaining quiet but watchful, even when he handed over a bundle of Nepalese Rupee notes and what appeared to be travel documents of some kind to a couple of official-looking men. She stayed quiet, even when he shepherded her, Rohan held safely in her arms, into a rickshaw and they rattled across the Mechi River bridge, the boundary between Nepal and India. She even managed to stay silent when she glanced over her shoulder at her native country one last time, not realizing that it would be more than two and a half years before she and Rohan would see Nepal again.

Once on the Indian side, it was a short bus ride to Siliguri Railway Station. Radhika was exhausted but she had to keep alert for Rohan, but the noise and bustle of this new place was overwhelming. A travel hub nestling in the base of the Darjeeling hills, Siliguri is a rapidly developing, modern town located in the Darjeeling district of West Bengal state. It is famous for its beautiful natural surroundings and offers a splendid view of Kanchenjunga, the third highest mountain in the world after Mount Everest and K2 at 8,586m (28,169ft) high. Part of the impressive Himalaya mountain range, Kanchenjunga, which translates as 'the five treasures of snows', is believed to be sacred in the Kirant region. The 'treasures' are gold, silver, gems, grain and holy books and are meant to represent the five repositories of God. But for the most part, the magnificent surroundings largely passed Radhika and Rohan by.

When the journey came to an end, they were whisked onto a North East Frontier Railways train taking them onto their next unidentified destination. As Radhika boarded the train, this time settling Rohan as comfortably as she could, she tried to dismiss a feeling of impending doom as the train pulled away from the station yet again.

After what seemed like endless hours of falling in and out of restless and groggy sleep, her head jarring as she tried to keep awake, to keep focussed on what the next minutes would bring, the train finally jolted to a halt and Rajan Pariyar stood up, indicating that their journey had come to an end.

As she left the carriage, her eyes gritty with tiredness, her body weak from the months of malnutrition and the effects of having only one kidney, a brightly coloured sign caught Radhika's eye. She could just make it out. It read: 'WELCOME TO ASSAM' in Assamese and English. Before she could re-read it to confirm it wasn't all a dream, Radhika's travel companion forced her and Rohan into yet another rickshaw, grunting an address in the driver's ear.

Radhika didn't quite catch where they were going and probably wouldn't have been able to locate where they were on a map. She only knew that she was not in Nepal and that she and Rohan were far, far away from Parvati and her family and anyone else that knew her. Far, far away from the family she had yet to introduce Rohan to.

She shivered as she wondered what lay ahead for her and for her young son. And tried to ignore the growing certainty that whatever it was, it wasn't good.

They headed to the town of Silchar, in southern Assam. Advancements in education, medical facilities and, more recently, a booming real estate market have transformed the town. It attracts traders from distant parts of India and, as a result, in recent years, its population has grown to around 145,000 people. India's former Prime Minister Indira Gandhi once referred to it as an 'Island of Peace'. She regarded it as a very tranquil place in the otherwise turbulent north-east region.

But Radhika could not find peace anywhere. How could she when she wasn't at all sure what was going to happen next? Of course she had been lied to yet again by the Pariyars, but incredibly, Rajan still tried to maintain the façade that he was a friend helping her to find lucrative work – even though she hadn't actually asked him to. She remained cautious and distant, watching for what would happen next. Wherever she was going, it wasn't to the work he had promised, that much she was sure.

She was right to distrust him. Within half an hour of disembarking from the train, Radhika and Rohan had arrived at the destination that was about to become their 'home' for six months. Rajan had brought Radhika and her one-year-old son to a brothel.

Prostitution is big business in the state of Assam, although few visitors to the beautiful area, famous for its hill stations and tea, might suspect it. South of the Himalayas and the tiny kingdom of Bhutan, north of Bangladesh, Assam is a monsoon land. For years it was off-limits to tourists because of the insurgency in the area, generated by ethnic tension between the Bodo and Santhal tribes in western Assam, who have a history of bitter conflict. Now, adventurous Westerners and Indians alike delight in spending time there, looking at the elephants and great rhinoceroses native to the Kaziranga National Park and passing many a romantic night in the grand, converted former colonial tea estate houses.

But while wealthy Americans and Europeans sleep on ornate four-poster beds, a seedier side to Assam exists. The underbelly of the region is full of pimps, madames and prostitutes and a generation of young girls, many Nepalese in origin, are forced to sell their bodies to up to 30 clients a day on filthy, stinking mattresses in squalid conditions.

Every year, an average of 250 women and 200 girl children go missing in the state, disappearing to all extents and purposes into the ether. Some of the Assam Police believe that the majority are being trafficked for sex and this is a huge problem not just in India but worldwide as well. According to the United Nations (UN), about 2,500 women and children around the world 'disappear' every day to be sold into sex slavery. Some are more valuable commodities than others. Nepalese girls are particularly favoured in India because of their light skins and trusting natures.

These young Nepalese are isolated because they do not speak the local dialect and have no family locally. This makes it much easier to keep them in line. According to Maiti Nepal, the Kathmandu refuge for trafficked women and children, a large percentage of children are trafficked into the sex trade by the owners of factories, who lure them away from villages with the promise of lucrative jobs. Some are sold from such villages by parents who want money to educate their sons (in such cases, boys are viewed as far more important than girls, who are dispensable). Others are sold to brothels by husbands who have taken teenage brides for this exact purpose.

Most girls have no inkling that they will end up in a brothel. When they discover their fate, a few find the courage to fight.

In many cases, they learn their lesson quickly: gang rapes, beatings and torture quickly pacify them and make them more willing to accept the 'clients' who come to see them. A few still bide their time, waiting for a chance to escape, believing that they can and some do. In most cases, however, they are caught, returned by the taxi-drivers, shop owners or countless others, who are often in league with brothel keepers and thus return them to their 'homes'.

Some continue to try to escape, dreaming of their former lives or future better lives. After the next time they are caught, or the time after that, after further rapes, beatings and threats, eventually they get the message and most learn to accept their life.

And what is life for them?

Certainly, financial rewards are not forthcoming. A large slice of a trafficked girl's earnings are withheld to repay the brothel owner for her own purchase price. 'Expenses', such as the price of food, clothing, bedding, medical bills for sexually transmitted diseases (STDs) or abortions, are often added onto this sum at exorbitant rates, and they also need to be repaid. As the debt increases, the girls grow older and less desirable to their clients and their earnings begin to fall, so the idea of buying their freedom, if that offer indeed exists, recedes.

The police sometimes raid the brothels and jail the sex workers along with pimps, madames and traffickers, but again there is little hope of escape for many of these young women. Corruption permits this lucrative sex industry to thrive, and some officials, police, council workers and others – the very people who are meant to protect the innocent and vulnerable – are among those who use the brothels in the first place.

In the rare cases when a Nepalese woman succeeds in escaping from a brothel or is deemed too old for the tastes of the clients or is discarded because she is riddled with a venereal disease or with HIV/AIDS, she may make it back across the border from India to Nepal, but the reception that awaits her may make her wonder why she tried.

Once home, such women are often ostracized by society at large and by family, even in the cases where the latter has been complicit in helping prostitute its women folk. A family who has bought a house through selling a daughter to a brothel may refuse her admittance to that same home for a variety of reasons.

Many villagers believe that if you inhabit the same house as someone who has HIV, you will become infected, for example. Others still refuse to be in the same room as someone so dishonorable, a fallen woman, even though they may have themselves brought about her downfall.

Hypocrisy is rife everywhere, it seems.

Radhika's introduction to the world of prostitution was slow, subtle and devious. Within seconds of stepping out of the rickshaw outside the building, a heavily made-up woman greeted her and Rohan warmly as they stood outside a three-storey building in a rundown street. It was still daylight and Radhika's attention was caught by the huge crowd of men in the house and the women, some young girls, dressed in very little, many hanging rather provocatively off balconies.

Barely knowing what to think Radhika clutched Rohan to her, burying his head in her shoulder. Another woman, dressed in a yellow sari, greeted them. She had long greasy hair and she wore cheap heels, heavy make-up and, to Radhika's eyes at least, far too many bangles. Even the accessories in her hair looked tacky. She appeared to know Rajan but it was clear from her manner that they weren't friends or intimates.

The woman spoke to Radhika in Nepali, introducing herself as Rupa Tamang. Radhika was surprised as she had never come across women like this before. They remained outside, exchanging a few pleasantries and for the first time since she began the journey, Radhika began to relax slightly. Perhaps it wouldn't be that bad after all. Perhaps her experiences had just made her mistrustful of everyone.

A man then appeared, who Rupa Tamang introduced as her husband. He told Radhika that he would return the next day to help her start looking for a job. That's when Radhika's fear returned, but she had little choice but to go along with them.

They led the way into the house. Inside it looked just as it had from the outside: it was dingy and dilapidated. The paucity of windows meant that it was quite dark, the lack of natural light exacerbated by the shadows of the neighbouring buildings. The house was in the middle of a densely populated and built-up area. The green fields and blue skies that Radhika had savoured on the way to Assam were now a thing of the past. She mentally shook herself. She was determined as ever to make the best of her lot and vowed to spruce the place up. If this was to be home for her and Rohan she would do her best to make it feel that way.

For some reason, the room that Radhika was given was separated from the rest of the house, which she thought odd but she didn't say anything. She was grateful to have somewhere for her and Rohan to finally lay their heads. There was no one to talk to but it was enough that she had Rohan as a constant companion. Permanently glued to Radhika's hip, he seemed a little bewildered by his new surroundings but he was happy enough when his mother was around. The room they shared was small and windowless with no air conditioning and the March heat was stifling. It was situated on the ground floor of the building and lay adjacent to the Tamangs' living quarters. Brown paint peeled off the otherwise bare walls and greasy cooking smells permeated the stagnant air.

Occasionally, Radhika could make out the sounds of raised voices through the wooden walls. There was also a lot of music, but it didn't disturb her. If anything the noise was comforting, proving that she wasn't alone.

On the first morning there, she had risen early, anxious to find out what job awaited her, only to be told to relax and not to worry about looking for a job so early in her stay. Her new employers implied that she should look on them as surrogate parents and told her that they would be happy to accommodate her and Rohan until a suitable job became available. Despite her initial misgivings, in those first days Radhika found life so easy, so undemanding for her and Rohan. She had prepared herself for what might come – hard labour at best, prostitution at worst, but strangely she was being left alone. She thought about that constantly, dreamed about it. She wasn't stupid and over the days, her initial belief that she was living in a brothel had been proved right. She simply couldn't fathom why she wasn't being forced to join the other girls in selling her body, but she was so thankful that she couldn't bring herself to question why she was different.

Radhika's life appeared to be unfolding in a sequence of incomprehensible events. But as long as Rohan was safe and happy she wasn't about to rock the boat. So, when the Tamangs finally asked her do some light cleaning chores around the place she was happy to do so and it meant that she could keep Rohan near her. In return, Radhika was fed a protein-rich diet of fish, meat, eggs and juice, which was delicious but initially very hard to digest after her enforced diet of endless vegetables. She even happily accepted the tuition she was offered on how to put on make-up, how to style her hair, what to wear, how to walk properly, things that she had never been able to do with her sisters or mother. And she hadn't really had any friends to do such things with either.

So, Radhika and Rohan wiled away the time over the days and weeks that followed, building up their strength and largely being allowed to sleep and play simple hide-and-seek games, the kind of things that she hadn't been allowed to do when she was a child.

Perhaps, Radhika thought, her luck had finally changed, and it was just the horrible experiences of the last two years that had made her so cynical. Maybe Lakshmi was with her again and Rajan had really wanted to help her, taking her here rather than to her sister in Kathmandu, because he knew it would be better for her and Rohan in the end. Perhaps she had finally met some good and genuine people, employers who wanted to help make her strong before finding her a good job. *Perhaps.* But niggling doubts, which she did her very best to suppress, kept her awake at night.

Sadly Radhika's hopes that her life had changed for the better were unfounded, only her doubts had some basis. The eight weeks of rest and recuperation that the Tamangs allowed her were all part of an intricate and ruthlessly executed plan to make Radhika fit and attractive enough for her new job as a prostitute.

She recalls, 'I was blissfully ignorant [of] the fact that I was about to embark on a dangerous and soul-destroying game of Russian roulette.

'The fact that I have lived to tell the tale is a miracle.

'If it hadn't have been for Rohan and my intense love for him, I would have put a gun to my head and pulled the trigger [myself].'

'Dhanda'
must begin

WITHOUT any warning whatsoever, Rupa Tamang burst into the room, disturbing the laughter-filled game of hide-and-seek Radhika was playing with 14-month-old Rohan. She stared at Radhika for a few brief seconds before announcing: *'Dhanda* must begin.'*

Shocked by the woman's odd behaviour, Radhika asked Rupa Tamang what she meant. She was stunned. Gone was the previously kind and thoughtful woman who had all but taken her and Rohan under her wing, instead stood this hard-faced, menacing stranger.

Radhika recalls, 'I asked what kind of business she was talking about and she told me crossly to shut up. [She] began painting my face.... [She told me] it was time to get ready to stand outside the building.'

The unthinkable had finally happened. Radhika had been lulled into a false sense of security. She had actually believed that her luck had changed and that she might be able to give Rohan the life he deserved. But Rupa Tamang had finally revealed her true colours. Once again, Radhika had put her trust in someone unworthy of her.

*Dhanda literally translates as 'business' in Hindi but its more colloquial usage relates to prostitution.

Radhika's life as a prostitute was about to start. As Rupa Tamang had informed her: *'Dhanda must begin'* – no matter how hard she might try to fight it.

The demand for prostitutes such as Radhika in economically booming towns like Silchar is great.

Situated by the banks of the Barak River in what is popularly known as Barak Valley, Silchar has tremendous commercial importance as the second largest town in the state of Assam. It attracts ambitious traders from distant parts of India. Real estate flourishes, alongside commercial businesses, making the city attractive to those seeking to make their fortune.

Young men flock to the area, seeking work and new opportunities. Single or just away from their families, these men, alone in a new place, seek what comfort they can, wherever they can, particularly if it's with a young, pretty and available girl.

Human traffickers have been quick to take advantage of the benefits of the changing socio-demographics of places like Silchar. It's an easy market in which to sell young girls into prostitution and innocent Nepalese girls are particularly popular with clients.

There are plenty of Silchar men able to afford the pitiful 200 Indian Rupees (£2.89) price tag for sex after a hard day's work. It doesn't really matter to most of them if that girl is willing or not. Nor are they interested in the story of how that young girl came to be selling her body. They've paid for their pleasure after all and that's *all* that matters.

Overleaf: Radhika with her son, Rohan.
Above: Radhika's mother, Maiya Phuyal, at home.

Above: Radhika's father, Ramprasad Phuyal.

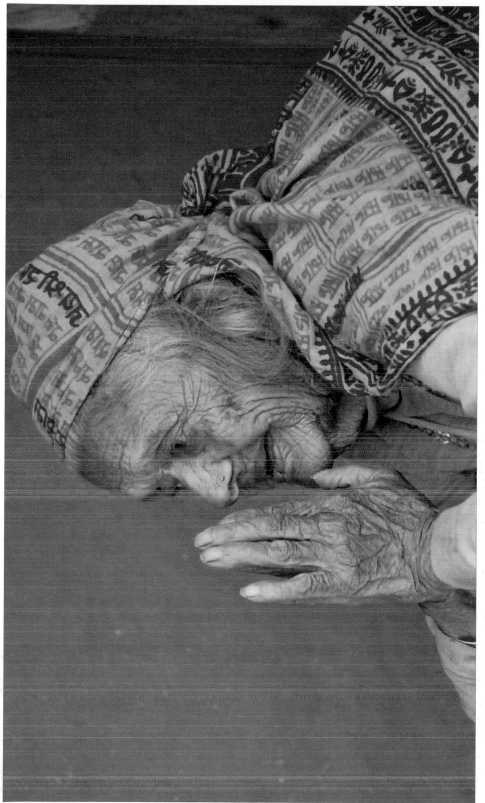

Above: Radhika's paternal grandmother, Hari Prem.

Above: Radhika's family outside their home in Kavresthali. Back L–R: Radhika, Parvati Khatiwada (Radhika's eldest sister); Bal Krishna (Radhika's brother); Nani Maiya (Radhika's youngest sister). Front L–R: Ramprasad (Radhika's father); Hari Prem (Radhika's grandmother); Rohan and Maiya (Radhika's mother).

*Above: The Balaju Vegetable Market,
where Radhika's trafficking nightmare began.*

*Above: Chennai railway station, to which Radhika's captors took her after drugging her and
before taking her to a nearby hospital, where a doctor was on standby to remove her kidney.*

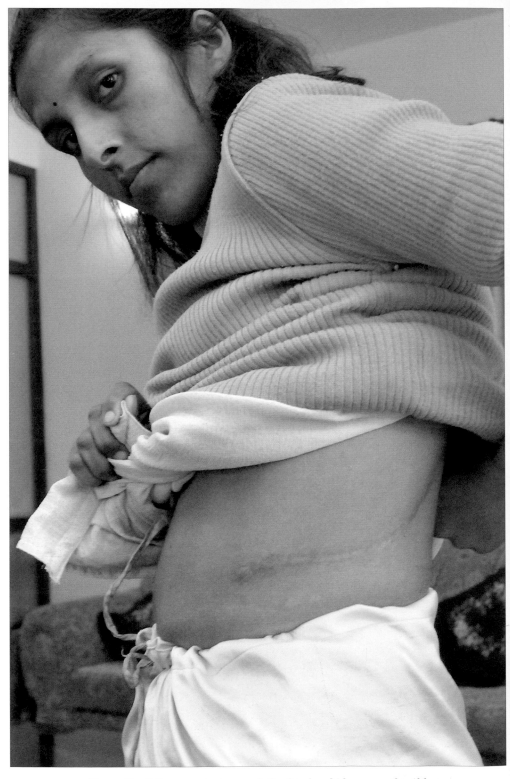

Above: Radhika reveals the scar left after her kidney was forcibly removed from her body in a Chennai hospital.

Left: Sindhupalchowk, a deprived province 20km northeast of Kathmandu, where Radhika's husband, Rajesh, insisted they set up home after their marriage. Rohan was born here.

Overleaf: Radhika with Rohan outside her family home in Kavresthali. She is not allowed inside because she married beneath her caste.

Above: Krishna 'Purne' Pariyar is one of the men who trafficked Radhika. In June 2010 he was given a four-year prison sentence under the Human Trafficking Act B.S. 2064 (2007–2008 A.D.).

Right: Lakshmi: the Hindu goddess of wealth and prosperity to whom Radhika often prayed.

Above: Trains were key to Radhika's experiences in India — not just because they transported her to and from the brothels, where she was forced to work as a prostitute, but also because on these trips she was reunited with her beloved son, Rohan.

Above: Central Jail, Tripureswor, Kathmandu, where Rajan Pariyar and Krishna 'Purne' Pariyar were held on trafficking charges before their conviction in June 2010.

Opposite: Maiti Nepal founder, Anuradha Koirala.

Above: The Maiti Nepal refuge, which Radhika and Rohan now call home.

Left: Radhika, and other girls at the refuge, making beaded bracelets in the Maiti Nepal workshop.

Above: Radhika, Rohan and other child survivors of human trafficking.

*Above: Radhika and Rohan with her family
on a trip back to her native village.*

*Above: A radiant Radhika and Rohan sit with Radhika's
grandmother and father outside the family home.*

Above: Radhika's father, Ramprasad, with Rohan.

Above: Radhika's youngest sister, Nani Maiya, with Rohan.

Above: Rohan with Radhika and her mother.

Overleaf: Radhika and Rohan – in much happier times.

Above: Sharon Hendry (right) interviews Radhika's 102-year-old grandmother, Hari Prem (far left), with the help of translator, Elisha (middle).

Radhika's life was slowly descending into a nightmare of epic proportions. But outweighing even the fear of what might happen to her was what might happen to Rohan. If she wasn't around, who would keep him safe?

A hard-faced looking, plump Bengali woman in her early 20s appeared in the doorway to Radhika and Rohan's room and told her that she had come to take the boy away. A feeling of terror formed a vice-like grip around Radhika's throat, making her breathing short and shallow. This wasn't happening? This *couldn't* happen. Rohan was too small to be separated from her. He couldn't cope without her. *She* couldn't cope without *him*. They were all each other had.

Radhika's sense of betrayal and humiliation were overwhelming. She had truly come to believe that Rupa Tamang was on her side. Radhika glanced at her son, who was crouching down on the floor, contentedly humming a tune, unaware of the undercurrents in the room running between Radhika, the Bengali woman and Rupa Tamang.

'Rohan ... had just started learning to crawl. He was a very late developer. This was possibly because of his traumatic birth, when the umbilical chord had been wrapped around his neck and possibly because of the terrible upheaval he had experienced in his very short life.

'[N]ow he was developing a real awareness of the world around him. I knew he would be ... aware of being wrenched away from me... [I]t still makes me feel sick to reflect on the terror he must have felt.

'I began pleading with them, trying to persuade them that I could take care of Rohan and work at the same time but

Rupa [just] barked [at me]: "Shut up, you cannot work and be a mother. We will bring Rohan to you frequently."'

Shock and fear quickly turned to debilitating grief as Radhika finally understood that this was the reality of her situation and there was nothing she could do.

She began to sob uncontrollably, her slender body convulsing as she tried to make sense of what was happening. After everything she had endured in the past few years, Rohan was her 'bright star', the one truly good thing in her life and her reason for living. He had brought light and hope back to her at her time when it seemed her life was over, even though she had only been 17 at the time. He made her stronger and allowed her to believe that there was a better future for both of them.

Like many Nepalese mothers, Radhika had always kept Rohan physically close to her. When he wasn't strapped tightly to her back in bright swathes of swaddling material, he was sharing a small bed with her, feeling his mother's warm, reassuring breath on his tiny face each night as he closed his eyes and, again, each morning when he opened them. How would they survive without one another?

Since his birth, Radhika had never spent more than an hour apart from her beloved son. How could she be separated from him?

By now hysterical, Radhika tried to calm herself down. She tried to be rational, comprehending that this was the only way in which she might get answers to her questions. Rupa Tamang promised Radhika that Rohan was going to a wonderful safe place, where he would be well looked after alongside lots of other children. She told Radhika that she would see him once a week, but Radhika instinctively knew that she was being lied to.

She recalls, 'I could tell by her eyes that the truth was more painful and sinister. Her stare was cold and hard. She started screaming at me, telling me not to argue, before slapping me round the face. She told me I would be killed if I didn't go along with the plan.'

Radhika realized that there was no way out. That she had no choice other than to go along with whatever these women wanted if she were to keep Rohan safe and herself alive.

She walked slowly across the room and scooped her young son up into her arms. Clutching him close, she soaked up the boy's familiar sweet smell, nuzzling his face as she whispered in his ear so low that only he could hear, 'I love you and I will come for you. Never, ever forget me.'

Rohan knew that something was wrong. He looked into Radhika's soft dark eyes and began to sob deep, animalistic cries of grief that seemed to come from the depths of his soul.

'The sound still haunts me to this day,' Radhika says.

But it wasn't over yet. Radhika couldn't bear to hand him over and eventually it was left to the Bengali woman to take him. She did so brutally and without compassion, lunging towards mother and child and ripping Rohan aggressively from Radhika's arms. She turned abruptly on the heels of her cheap red fashion shoes and muttered to Radhika that she would bring him to visit her once a week, before she disappeared into the humid afternoon with Radhika's bright star held roughly in her arms.

Radhika fell backwards and her frail body began to slide slowly down the roughly plastered wall.

'How can I describe the feeling?,' she says, 'Except to say my whole world had been taken away, my life blown apart ... to take Rohan was the equivalent of ripping out my heart. I wanted to kill myself, to end my life there and then but I had to keep fighting for survival. I vowed to do whatever it took to get Rohan back.'

But there was little time for Radhika to grieve over the loss of her son. *Dhanda* must begin. All Radhika could do was hope that Rohan would be cared for properly – and that this also hadn't been a lie.

It is difficult to give exact figures for the amount of trafficked women who become prostitutes in Silchar or Assam, but as a point of reference, the red light district in Mumbai is the biggest in the world and generates at least 18,758,755,343.01 INR (about £277 million) a year in revenue. It houses 100,000 prostitutes servicing men 365 days a year and averaging 6 customers a day, at 93 INR (£1.34) each. Ninety per cent are indentured slaves, with as many as half trafficked from Nepal, according to human rights groups*. It's a lucrative business, which is equal to, or at times exceeds, the drugs trade.

For those trafficked with children, the fate of their young is equally bleak. The women's reassurances that Rohan would be well cared for were nothing more than barefaced lies. An untold number of children live in the brothel areas of India – untold because so many are hidden below the official radar. Some are born in captivity; others, like Rohan, are trafficked with their mothers.

Anuradha Koirala, the founder of the Kathmandu-based refuge for trafficked women Maiti Nepal (Mother's Home)

*Robert I. Freidman, 'India's Shame: Sexual Slavery and Political Corruption are Leading to an AIDS Catastrophe,' *The Nation,* 8 April 1996.

explains, 'When a mother is trafficked with a child, the brothel owners don't want the mother to be disturbed so they immediately separate them. The so-called "crèches" are usually near the brothels (but of course the mothers are not told this) and typically there are 2 or 3 women looking after 20 to 30 children. The rooms are small, dirty and dingy and the children are fed a basic diet of rice and a few vegetables. They have nothing to play with and sleep next to one another on small, filthy mats on the floor.

'Doctors are never used when the children are sick unless the conditions are reported. At best, a local "quack" will see a desperately ill child. Generally, the children have to be quiet at all times and their cries are silenced by making them sick. The crèche supervisors – who are of course part of the trafficking gangs – either burn their tongues or genitals with cigarettes. The idea is to make the child become so subdued or sick, it no longer cries for its mother.

'Many children lie there moaning at first and ... a percentage become mute through the trauma of their experience.'

Radhika's chest hurt from sobbing.

She crouched down in the corner of the dingy room she had been sharing with Rohan for the past weeks and began to apply the garish make-up that Rupa Tamang had thrown so aggressively at her.

Now she knew the real meaning behind the lessons that the woman had given her to help her look more feminine. Once, she had convinced herself that it was no more than girlish fun and actually enjoyed them, but now she knew the truth – that she was being shown how to show herself off to the best advantage in order to sell sex.

In silence, Radhika used a small, broken hand mirror to apply each product. First, she applied thick, black kohl to accentuate her striking, arched eyebrows; then, she slicked a thick green eye shadow across her lids, before making the final transformation from innocent village girl to brazen woman with a slash of blood-red lipstick. With each stroke of the make-up brush, Radhika felt her identity slipping further away. She watched as a stranger, harder, more worldly image appeared. This wasn't her.

Finally, she pulled on the 'uniform' Rupa Tamang had provided her with. She felt self-conscious, almost naked in the shell pink lace bra and matching French knickers and negligee, which in other circumstances she might have enjoyed. She was now frightened of the opposite sex, learned through her bitter experience with Pariyar, the drunk and violent lower-caste husband she had been forced to marry, and also the sex traffickers who had brought her to this place. She had never learned how to feel desired or desirable, only worthless and unwanted. And the short black skirt and cheap pink heels that she was required to wear to tout for *Dhanda* only served to lower her rock bottom self-esteem still further. As she watched in the mirror, her transformation into a seductive slum hooker was complete.

'Of course, people have asked why I didn't just run away. But isn't it obvious?' Radhika cries.

'The traffickers had kidnapped my son and knew I wouldn't leave without him.

'What better way of enslaving a mother?

'Now I was about to pay a ransom bigger and more terrible than [anyone] could ever have imagined.'

'DHANDA' MUST BEGIN

Radhika shuffled awkwardly down the passageway, her new shoes making it difficult for her to walk properly with her head held low. She came to know the passageway as the 'catwalk', somewhat ironic as its appearance was a far cry from the glossy fashion plinths of Paris and Rome. The 'catwalk' is, in fact, where the prostitutes of India's slum districts are forced to tout their wares.

Finally, she came to stand in front of the old blue plastic chair which was to be her stall. Radhika cleared her throat before uttering the vile, sugary phrase that Rupa Tamang had made her repeat over and over again: *'Chalo mere saath, chalo mere saath* (Hindi for 'Come with me, come with me").

She tried to go through the motions and whisper the words seductively but all she ocould think of was Rohan. Where was he? What was he doing? Was he OK? Had he stopped crying yet? Was someone holding him? She was almost numb with grief.

It was around an hour before Radhika was forced to entertain her first client. The experience is still vivid for her and marked by the haunting sound of a door latch clicking shut. She says, 'I don't think I will ever forget that sound, so simple but chilling and horribly suffocating.

'The man picked me out of a group of girls on the catwalk, saying he liked my light skin and slender frame. Then he followed me inside the building. I tried to pretend I was someone else, an actress playing a part in a film.

'He was fat, dark and scary and he forced himself on me within seconds, throwing me down on the mattress while trying to rip off my underpants. But I instinctively fought him off and managed to run out of the room screaming and shaking. I was met by the brothel owner Rupa Tamang. She grabbed me by the hair and said: "You have been sold and you are worthless to everyone except me …There is no choice if you want to see your son again." She forced me back in again.… [T]hat was my first client. He abused me in every way imaginable, forcing me to perform oral sex and endure anal sex. All the while, the smell of alcohol and sweat seeped out of his pores. It's all about the customers' satisfaction in the slum brothels. As a person, you cease to exist. And that's what I had to learn fast.

'I began to perfect the art of detaching my mind from my body but I still remember thinking to myself: "This is the end of everything – the end of my life as I know it."'

At first, Radhika was forced to sleep with up to 15 clients a day. Towards the end of the six-month period she spent in Assam, it increased to between 20 and 30 per day. The price tag was a mere 200 INR (£2.89) per client for full sex. Few wanted to wear protection but Radhika says Rupa Tamang insisted on it, but this was not out of concern for her employees' welfare. She was far more worried about dead or desperately ill girls destroying profit margins.

Some clients compromised Radhika's soul, others threatened her life. Over the months she had many encounters but one in particular stuck in her mind. A young man who appeared to be from a wealthy background picked Radhika out from the catwalk parade. He was well-dressed and well-spoken. They had sex but when he suggested having anal sex and Radhika refused, his mood quickly turned sour. Suddenly, he produced a large kitchen knife and lunged forward trying to stab her.

Hysterical, Radhika ran out into the street in just her bra and pants and screamed and screamed. All she could think about was Rohan and what would happen to him if she wasn't there one day to rescue him from the people who had captured them. When the police eventually came all that happened was that the girls inside the brothel were rounded up by Rupa Tamang and hidden in a tunnel behind a staircase. Many of the policemen were familiar faces anyway, because some were clients while others took bribes from Tamang to allow her to continue trading.

In the long months that Radhika spent selling her body and soul on the seedy mattresses of Assam, she didn't see her son. Her captors, far from keeping their promise, did not allow her to see her cherished little boy and enquiries about Rohan were routinely met with violent slaps and cigarette burns on her arms and legs. All that kept her going was the notion that one day she might be reunited with Rohan, so she bore the slaps and the burns, and continued to ask when she might see him.

And then, one day, her prayers were answered – but not in the way she had hoped for. A new associate of Rupa Tamang's appeared at the brothel, an 18-year-old named Raju Tamang, who had been assigned to transport Radhika to a new town. Despite sharing the same surname, Rupa and Raju did not appear to be related although Radhika suspects they hailed from the same village somewhere in Nepal.

Radhika says: 'Tamang told me I would be going to Kolkata (Calcutta) because the business there was better. The day I was due to leave, the Bengali woman suddenly appeared with Rohan. I ran to him and threw my arms around him, ruffling his hair and kissing his tiny face but, heartbreakingly I seemed to be a stranger to him and he began clinging to the Bengali woman's neck.

'He was desperately confused and now considered her to be his mother. He looked healthy and was dressed in a clean pair of jeans and a T-shirt but I felt utterly helpless. My own son didn't recognize me and it seemed like he was lost to me forever. But there was no time to dwell on anything. Once more, my precious little boy and I were on the move.'

Given just half an hour to gather up her small plastic bag of belongings at Rupa Tamang's brothel, she prepared herself both mentally and physically for the arduous journey to Kolkata, some 518km (321 miles) south-west of Assam.

Dusk was falling as she hastily packed the cheap lace garments and garish make-up, which had become the tools of her soul-destroying trade, into a bag. Rohan sat watching his mother with a look of resignation. Despite the trauma he had clearly experienced, there were no tears, no tantrums. Worryingly, he had become mute.

Radhika says: 'When Rohan was wrenched away from me ... was beginning to form words and sing songs. Now he said nothing at all. I sensed anger and terror in his expression. I suppose he still recognized me as his mother on one level but I hadn't done my job properly. I was supposed to be the person protecting him from harm's way and I had failed him miserably.

'I'm not surprised he was unwilling to trust me again. It was as if he was thinking exactly [the same thing as] I was: "We're together again – but for how long?"'

'I tried to ask the Bengali woman about Rohan and how he had been cared for but she told me nothing.

'She didn't have to. Rohan's sadness spoke volumes.'

All Radhika could do was cling to her son, even though the boy didn't seem to want to acknowledge her as his mother.

Sonagachi song

RAJU Tamang, a thin, wiry boy with greasy black hair who always wore fake designer sunglasses, accompanied Radhika and Rohan on the gruelling trek from Silchar to Kolkata.

The bus journey lasted two nights and one day and Raju's role was crucial. He was to make sure that his precious cargo reached its new destination. With her clean good looks, pale Nepalese skin and innocent and, for the most part, compliant nature, Radhika was far too lucrative a trafficking commodity to risk losing along the way.

But far from complaining, Radhika savoured every second of the tiresome journey. Resigned once more to her terrible fate, she held Rohan so close that he could hardly breathe. It felt good to drink in the milky softness of his skin and run her fingers through his glossy black hair.

For the two nights they travelled together, Radhika stayed awake just so she could watch her tiny son breathing. She knew his innocence was slowly slipping away thanks to the terrible vortex of crime that the pair had been sucked into. But here, asleep in her arms, Rohan was the same sweet child she had given birth to on the floor of a clay house in March 2004. And in her dreams, she was the same perfect mother who vowed always to protect her child against all the odds.

The screech of a decrepit set of brakes jolted Radhika out of her deep thoughts. The bus had reached its destination and before she knew it her time with Rohan was over. Raju rushed them off the bus and was hastily arranging a taxi to pack his prized packages into before they could blink.

Radhika comments, 'This time I asked no questions and revealed no emotion. I had a good idea of what fate had in store for Rohan but I could not bring myself to think of being separated from him again. In just 48 hours, he had begun to know me as his mother once more. If we were ripped apart again, it might break us [this time].'

After another gruelling two-hour taxi ride, first through countryside, then more densely populated suburbs, and finally, into the jaws of the sprawling city of Kolkata. Radhika and Rohan stepped out onto the roadside and glanced up at their new home. This time there was no mistaking the brothel that was about to become Radhika's new home.

A dilapidated four-storey structure, the building looked even more uninviting than the previous brothel had done to Radhika, all that time ago when Rajan Pariyar had dropped her off there. It sat in shameful contrast to many of the city's buildings, which are fabulous in their architecture and historic importance.

The West Bengali city of Kolkata (formerly Calcutta) served as the capital of the British Raj in India until 1912. Many of the city's buildings are adorned with Gothic, Baroque, Roman, Oriental and Indo-Islamic motifs. And several major buildings of the colonial period are well maintained and have been declared 'heritage structures', while others are in various stages of decay.

Radhika's new 'home' was beyond decay. Rotting wood formed the foundations that served to shakily support layers of pen-like rooms and tiny windows were only for show at the front of the building. Those girls forced to live in the middle and at the back of the house were starved of air, forced to drink in the stale, sweat-soaked oxygen from morning till night.

Anyone lucky enough to occasionally glimpse the street scenes outside would find themselves immersed in the type of chaos that has to be seen to be believed. Kolkata currently has a population exceeding 15 million, making it the third most populous metropolitan area in India and one of the most populous urban areas in the world.

The city is also classified as the eighth largest urban agglomeration in the world. For simple, country girls like Radhika, it was utterly alien and unnerving. The mere sight of it, in fact, caused a knot to form instantly in the pit of Radhika's stomach.

She was right to feel afraid. Her nose for danger was now much better, perhaps honed by her six months in Silchar and the experiences that she had been forced to endure there. The place to which she had been brought was on a far different scale to Rupa Tamang's brothel. Situated in the infamous red light district in north Kolkata's Sonagachi area, it is a literal hell on earth for the many young female slaves forced to sell their bodies in its dark recesses.

Sonagachi translates as 'golden tree' in Bengali, but there is nothing remotely uplifting about the several hundred multi-storey brothels that dominate the skyline here. An estimated 10,000 sex workers are forced to work the 'catwalk' or the 'line' near the busy intersection of Chittaranjan Avenue, Shobha Bazar and Beadon Street. Just north of this vision of hell in all its splendour is the 19th-century Marble Palace. Still a working residence for Raja

Rajendra Mullick Bahadur and his family, it was built in 1835 by the Raja, a wealthy Bengali merchant with a passion for collecting works of art. The house continues to be a residence for his descendants. Raja Rajendra Mullick was the adopted son of Nilmoni Mullick, who built a Jagannath temple that predates Marble Palace, and still stands within the premises, but is only accessible to members of the family.

The house is adorned with a priceless array of Victorian furniture, large chandeliers, busts of kings and queens and paintings by such celebrated artists as Sir Joshua Reynolds, the 18th-century English portrait painter; Rubens, the 17th-century Flemish Baroque painter; and the Italian artist Titian, the most important member of the 16th-century Venetian school. Perhaps nothing better illustrates the disparity between India's rich and poor than the juxtaposition of this palace and its residents with its neighbouring inhabitants, who are slum prostitutes.

Radhika's new 'home' immediately conjured up for her an image of a prison within a slum and made the former brothel in Silchar, Assam look like a palace.

Radhika says: 'I went directly to the fourth floor and met the female *gharwali* or brothel owner. Maya Tamang was a fat, fair-skinned woman in her late 30s. She was dressed in an expensive yellow and green sari. I scanned her face for any sign of emotion but there was none. Her vacant look terrified me because I instinctively knew it meant she had become indifferent to the evils I was about to endure. I had seen this look before. At that point, Raju prepared to leave.

He looked me in the eye and gestured towards Tamang, simply saying: "She will teach you everything you need to know", before turning on his heels and disappearing into the chaotic street scene outside.

'Tamang greeted me briefly and asked me to confirm my name before immediately summoning another woman into the room. She was middle-aged and fat with long black hair and she had a large mole on her cheek. Her slanted eyes suggested to me that she was from the Himalaya region of Nepal. It depressed me to meet yet another of my country's "sisters" who had turned against her own people. I knew immediately by the way they both looked at Rohan, what her role was going to be.'

Radhika was learning fast. As in the previous brothel, Rohan's presence was considered a distraction from *dhanda*. The modus operandi of the slum brothel owners was to remove any children from their workers. This not only enabled the girls to function more efficiently, but also gave the Madames something to hold over the girls.

This time Radhika watched as her son was taken away from her for the second time in his life. She couldn't speak or move, so heart-wrenching was it to watch him go. He didn't put up a fight. There was no sobbing or screaming like the first time they had parted. He just followed his new 'surrogate mother' silently out of the room with his head bowed. He had developed an unhealthy trust in strangers and it broke Radhika's heart to witness it. As he disappeared from view, she felt the blood rushing to her head and a loud ringing noise in her ears. Her legs gave way beneath her and she collapsed on the floor.

A sharp tug on her wrist jolted Radhika back to harsh reality. She barely had time to wipe the tears and mucus from her face before Maya Tamang, the Sonagachi brothel owner, was barking orders into her face.

In a low, masculine-sounding voice, she began to familiarize her latest slave with the house rules. 'Listen carefully. At 8 a.m., you will be ready for work. You will stand outside and lure the customers in. Take lunch briefly at 1 p.m., tea at 3 p.m. and dinner at 8 p.m. You will have meat every three days and rice and dhal in between. You must aim to entertain up to 30 clients per day and charge them 200 INR each (£2.89). All tips must be handed to me. Now follow me to your room. *HURRY!*"

Maya Tamang led Radhika to a small room comprising four cubicles, each separated by a set of filthy black and white curtains. At least there was the luxury of a window at one end of this rectangular shaped cell, but the stench of sex and sweat overpowered Radhika and for a moment she felt faint again.

Next, Radhika was introduced to her new roommates. She estimated that the three pretty Nepalese girls were aged between 14 and 18 years old, like Radhika. She found them frightening – a sign of what might happen to her if she let it – their blank expressions and sullen eyes suggested that their spirits had already been broken by the horrors that they had been forced to bear. She was determined that would not happen to her, that she would always fight, for Rohan's sake, if not her own. Radhika was to learn that each of the girls' stories were painfully similar to her own. They had been innocent village girls, like heself, but were lured into the sex trade by the promise of a good job and a better life.

Occasionally they spoke of escaping but Radhika knew that it was just an impossible dream: they were situated on the fourth floor of the building about 25m (82ft) off the ground. And besides, there were security guards crawling all over the brothel. There was also the Madame. Radhika was to learn that this particular women had a sadistic love of violence.

At random times during the day, the girls would brace themselves for a beating the moment they heard her plastic flip-flops squeaking down the corridor. Tamang took great pleasure in punishing the girls for what she saw as minor infringements of the house rules. Those who disobeyed the slightest decree would find themselves crushed under the blow of her favourite weapon – a heavy iron pipe that was wielded expertly even in her flabby arms.

Radhika endured many such beatings for failing to meet her 30-a-day client target. And she still bears the scars of cigarette burns inflicted on her by Tamang for the slightest disagreement. More shockingly, Tamang once poured boiling hot water down Radhika's back after she dared to answer her back on one occasion. The subject of the argument was so futile, Radhika still can't recall it.

All of this meant that the consequences of the discovery of a plot to escape or an unsuccessful escape simply didn't bear thinking about. And then there was Rohan. Rohan. About whose whereabouts she had absolutely no idea.

Radhika was also to learn quickly that there are violent men everywhere and the Kolkata brothel's clientele was particularly brutal. One of Radhika's first encounters with a client was horrific. The man was so drunk he could barely stand. He threw Radhika onto the bed before he kicked her so hard with his leather boots that he left a nasty scar on her right shin. She still bears it to this day.

The routine that the girls had to endure was also relentless. After every customer, their make-up had to be reapplied and Maya Tamang even forced them to carry on working while they were menstruating, although many of the girls stopped having periods altogether because they were so exhausted.

Physically, the work was beginning to take its toll on Radhika's body, even though she was only in her late teens. Her kidney scar was causing her a lot of pain, a grim reminder of how this had all begun. Occasionally customers would ask how she had got it and she would make up various stories about problems in childbirth.

But no physical pain inflicted on Radhika could match the mental torture she was suffering.

Rohan dominated Radhika's thoughts from dusk until dawn. Where was he? Where were they keeping him this time? Was he talking again? Or still mute? Did he lie awake at night and cry for her?

While prostitution was slowly destroying her body, the separation from Rohan was undeniably worse, tearing apart her soul.

After two months of continual pleadings, Radhika was eventually granted a 15-minute audience with Rohan. Heartbreakingly, at 20 months he was walking – having taken his first steps without his proud mother there to witness them.

Radhika says: '[Rohan's] new "carer" led him into a side room near my bedroom. He was upright, walking confidently on his little legs. How could I ever have imagined I would miss that magical moment? Inside, my heart was shattered ... but I had to appear strong for Rohan.

'Everything in our lives had changed but I concentrated on Rohan's beautiful features. At least they were still the same, even though I knew how much he was hurting inside, too. He was still my gorgeous son. I wanted to scream from the rooftops so he could hear me say: "Please forgive me, Rohan ... one day you will know I had no choice but to endure this for our survival.

'I could only hope we would reach that point without too much being lost in the process. Of course I scooped him up into my arms and smothered him with kisses but this time I was prepared for his response, which was cold and detached.

'Who could blame him? What kind of mother allows her child to endure such fear and uncertainty?

'He didn't want to sit with me for too long because he no longer trusted me but I was horrified to notice he had an open wound on his forehead and he clearly had a fever. When I asked how the injury had occurred, the woman looking after him merely grunted and told me she had no idea. She said all children were clumsy and it was nothing to worry about. Obviously I thought otherwise but I was powerless to do anything.'

This was also the point at which Radhika realized that her son didn't respond to his birth name 'Roshan', meaning 'bright star' in Nepali, any more. His captors had changed it to the more Hindi and less-conspicious sounding 'Rohan' and that was the name he now answered to.

Even though Radhika today calls her son Rohan (also the name used for the purposes of this book, to avoid confusion) she says, 'It saddened me deeply because it was a sign that we no longer had any real control over our lives or identities. But he seemed more comfortable with the name so I resolved to go along with it – and still do to this day.

'Our 15 minutes together flew by in what seemed like seconds. I tried to keep Rohan close to me without smothering him and I hummed a tune from a Nepalese folk song we used to sing together.

'When it came to saying goodbye, I had to shut my emotions down in the same way my son had learned to. How much longer could we endure this hell?

'Would the gods intervene and save us or would it have to be down to me to find an inner strength?

'Our fate was now hanging precariously in the balance.'

Jigmi

HOPE briefly raised its head in the form of one of Radhika's clients, Jigmi. A night customer, Jigmi immediately stood out from Radhika's other regular customers not just because he was so handsome, but also because at 21, he was so much younger than the normal clientele, who tended to be middle-aged men. At 1.88m (6ft 2 ins), Jigmi was tall, dark – his shiny, black shoulder-length hair was always freshly washed and tucked neatly underneath a baseball cap – and lean. He also had good dress sense, favouring freshly laundered smart cotton shirts tucked into modern, low-slung jeans. The young man could easily have found a girlfriend to satisfy his needs, but for some reason, Jigmi had set his sights on Radhika instead.

It was late summer 2006 and Radhika had been at the Sonagachi brothel for about nine months. She was a popular worker and had got to know the needs and wants of her clientele well.

They were mostly lower-caste men, who liked to drink cheap liquor, usually spirits or the home brew made by the brothel owners. Most would come after work, in the early evening, and begin drinking. By the time they got to the 'catwalk', they were often so drunk it was a miracle they were able to stand up, let alone attempt to have sex.

117

For the most part, their appearance was unkempt and their personal hygiene poor. But by now Radhika had perfected the art of the zoning out when she was forced to have sex with these strangers.

'I would focus on a spot on the wall and transport myself into another world,' she says. 'That way, I didn't have to think about the clients' hideous body odour or the pungent alcohol vapour seeping through their spotty pores. I didn't have to worry about their two-day old stubble scraping against my cheekbones or being thrown around the bed like a rag doll. I didn't even have to worry about being sexually exploited in the worst ways possible. After all, it wasn't me on that bed it was someone else.

'But with Jigmi it was different.'

Jigmi arrived at Maya Tamang's rundown brothel one Friday evening. The hard-faced Madame immediately began fawning over him, offering him a chair and the standard shot of house whisky. She hollered at her girls to form a line in front of him. For Radhika and some of the other girls, the 'line' or 'catwalk' was always a humiliating and nerve-wracking experience. Each prostitute was required to dress up in her sex-slave uniform and sell her particular wares. In Radhika's case, this meant donning a tight, lime-green mini dress and garish red heels, which showcased her slim figure and long legs. She was also required to apply heavy and full make-up (usually lots of black kohl and red lipstick) before joining the line and adopting a provocative pose.

Like animals brought to sell at a market, the girls waited, some self-consciously, others wearily, to see who would be 'bought' first. In some cases, a collective sigh of relief could be heard when a particularly cruel-looking customer dismissed them all and staggered out of the brothel, muttering some expletive or other under his breath. Most times, however, the girls weren't so lucky and one of them would have to suffer the violence eked out by such a man, while the other girls did their best to shut out the screams.

On the night Jigmi appeared, Radhika was feeling more vulnerable than ever before. Some days she could just about get through, but mostly she couldn't get Rohan out of her head and the thought of what was happening to him. On days like these, she felt like killing herself so acute was her pain, her anguish and also guilt at the fact she had let him down by not being with him, not being able to hold him, not being able to protect him.

It was weeks since she had been granted a 15-minute visit with her little boy and she had no way of receiving any word of his well-being. Knowing she could not leave this sordid world without him meant that she was in a constant state of purgatory. She lived for the day that they would get out of here but on days like this she wondered if that time would ever come. If this was her life forever, would they ever be able to escape this living hell?

While all these thoughts whirred around in her mind, Radhika waited in line with the rest of the girls while Jigmi watched them. What finally got through to Radhika was the fact that Jigmi appeared as uncomfortable in the brothel as she felt. Unusually for a customer, he refused the complimentary whisky shot and instead stood up, shifting nervously from one foot to another while he glanced apologetically at the women in front of him. Eventually, he nodded his head gently in Radhika's direction and asked Maya Tamang how he should proceed.

As Radhika led the way up the narrow stairwell to her fourth-floor bedroom, Jigmi told her it was the first time he had visited a brothel. He apologized for his ineptitude. Even so, Radhika wasn't so sure: 'I'd heard other men say that, thinking I was stupid enough to swallow their lies.'

She also wondered if this were true, why such a handsome man would want to pay for a woman when he could get one so easily for free. What was his particular perversion?

'I wasn't ready to believe Jigmi straightaway but there were certainly signs that pointed towards him being more decent than most other men I'd encountered. He told me he had always harboured a fascination [about] sleeping with a Sonagachi prostitute and liked the idea of becoming more sexually experienced before he settled down to marry. He may well have been lying to me but I didn't really care. It was just a relief to be in the company of a sober man.

'I began to go through the motions of taking off my dress to reveal my pink lace pants and bra before lying back on the bed, but he told me to keep my clothes on and said he'd prefer to chat.'

No client had ever said this to Radhika before and her previous misgiving arose to the afore. 'I couldn't help thinking he was about to do something terrible to me … kill me. But he was true to his word.'

Jigmi told Radhika that he lived in an apartment near Sonagachi and worked in a call centre. He explained that he wasn't interested in a quick sexual fix but would prefer to pay the extra rupees required for a 'night customer' rate. So Maya Tamang charged him double the standard 200 INR

(£2.80) rate and he was given permission to stay the night with Radhika. He told the young woman that he was captivated by her beauty and gentle nature and wanted to know everything about her.

'His compliments made me feel embarrassed. It was so long since anyone had taken an interest in me as a person [but finally] I found myself pouring out my heart to him. I told him all about my family and how it was destroying me to think they might believe I was dead.

'I explained how I had been duped and trafficked and, of course, I told him all about Rohan and how I had to stay strong for him so that I could one day find him and rescue him. Jigmi just lay on the threadbare mattress in my room listening to me intently. He didn't even attempt to take advantage of me or raise the question of sex. Eventually, in the early hours of the morning, we both fell asleep lying next to one another, fully clothed.'

When Radhika woke early at around 5 a.m. the next morning, she shook Jigmi awake. He hurried towards the door, saying that he would be late for work. Then, as he was pushing back the curtain that separated Radhika's section of the room from her fellow prostitutes, he walked slowly back to the mattress where Radhika was still reclining and kissed her tenderly on the forehead, promising to come back soon.

Radhika says, 'It's hard to describe how I felt ... after so long working in brothels, my feelings had become numb but I definitely felt something different. Perhaps it was due to the fact that I'd had one of the best night's sleep in months. Probably nothing more than that, I told myself.'

Still, she tried to quell the hope that he would keep his word and return as he had promised. She had learned from bitter experience that hope had little place in her world.

True to his word, Jigmi returned at around the same time the following week – on a Wednesday in the early evening. Radhika tried to suppress her excitement. She knew Jigmi was different to the other men who visited her.

Although 19, Radhika had never known what it felt like to be loved by men other than her father or brothers – and that felt like so long ago. The first man she had deeply trusted after leaving home to live in Kathmandu, was Sanjay Lama. She had believed that he was a friend who had her best interests at heart when he promised to help her find work but he had ruthlessly deceived her, only seeing her as the lucrative donor of a kidney for his clients. Her husband Rajesh Kumar had simply seen her as a punch bag on which to vent his ugly temper and a means to making money quickly. And every man she had encountered since then had viewed her as a piece of flesh just to be bought and sold, not as a human being. Could Jigmi *really* be any different?

If he didn't want her for sex, what *did* he want her for? It had crossed Radhika's mind, at one point, that he could be an undercover policeman. But she thought that this was wishful thinking on her part. Jigmi was too gentle, too honest, too inexperienced to lie, she felt sure.

When Jigmi finally arrived at the brothel, his visit followed the same pattern as before. Once again he paid to stay the night and once again he told Radhika it was not necessary for them to have sex.

This time they talked about their respective homelands. Radhika reminisced about Nepal and Jigmi spoke of his love for India. He had been born and raised in a lower middle-class family in Kolkata but had blown his chances. He hadn't studied hard enough at school and now found himself working in a dead-end job. He said his boredom had caused him to start smoking hashish and he was worried his habit could spiral out of control if he didn't reign it in. He wanted more from life, he said. This struck a chord with Radhika.

Jigmi and Radhika discovered that they both harboured dreams of becoming better-educated and travelling to far-off lands like Europe and America. They also had a shared passion for music and dancing. Since her childhood, Radhika had been mesmerized by dance. When she was little, she would spend hours watching her older sisters perfect their elegant moves for their wedding dances, after which she would secretly skip off to the nearby fields and work on her own routine alone. Later, when living alone in Kathmandu, Radhika continued to dream, practising her steps in time to the Nepalese music played on a second-hand stereo given to her by a fellow market trader.

During his third overnight stay, Jigmi persuaded Radhika to dance for him. She shakily inserted her favourite Nepalese music cassette into an ancient tape player and pressed the 'Play' button. As the hypnotic notes began flowing out from the *damaha* (a Nepalese flat drum made of metal and wood), Radhika began twisting and turning with perfect poise. Adopting the same Indian classical dance poses as her Bollywood heroines, she seductively twirled her wrists and gyrated her waist until she was lost in an erotic dream world. Jigmi sat captivated, watching as her bright pink floor-length dress gracefully gathered speed, whirling faster and faster round the room.

In the midst of the dance, the downtrodden victim of the ruthless sex trafficking trade disappeared and a more dignified, regal young woman emerged as she was immersed in her dreams. Finally, as the music faded, Radhika was jolted back to reality. She stood looking down self-consciously at her bare feet on the dirty floorboards. Then she glanced up at Jigmi, who was spellbound. Something in his eyes indicated to Radhika that he believed he might be in love with her. He looked at her like the Bollywood heroes did just before they kissed their heroines at the end of the movies. She tried to dismiss the idea.

Then he spoke softly. His next words gave her hope.

'I'm going to help you to escape and find your son. Be ready at the same time tomorrow and we will leave here in the middle of the night.'

Why he would do this, risk his own life, to help a virtual stranger was beyond Radhika, but she knew this was her one chance to get herself and Rohan away. Despite the possible negative outcome, she accepted his help without any hesitation. Perhaps it was sign from the gods that her bad luck was finally ending.

By now, Maya Tamang had become suspicious of Jigmi. His interest in Radhika raised doubts as to his motives in visiting her. House rule dictated that no client was permitted more than three overnight stays. But in exchange for 600 INR (£8.40), Jigmi had managed to persuade the Madame to allow him one last night visit to Radhika.

He arrived at the brothel after work at around 7 p.m., immediately following Radhika to her room. He had planned that they would rest until 3 a.m., then make their way silently downstairs and leave via the front door. If any of the burly security guards employed by Maya Tamang tried to confront them, Jigmi would say that they were just going to buy liquor.

He was sure his reputation as a well-paying customer would afford him some bargaining power with them.

Radhika stuffed her meagre belongings – a pair of jeans, some shampoo, two kurta salwar and a precious photograph of Rohan – into Jigmi's rucksack and waited. At approximately 3 a.m., the pair crept quietly down the rotten, creaking staircase and along a tight passageway towards the front door of the brothel. Radhika was terrified someone would hear them but incredibly, the security guards were asleep and so the final escape into the world outside went as seamlessly as Jigmi had planned.

Breathing in the muggy night air of the red-light district, Radhika felt free for the first time in months. She recalls: 'I felt like a caged animal that had been released from captivity. Along the roadside, we walked past countless other girls being forced to sell their scrawny bodies. One or two caught my eye and seemed to sense that I was one of them. It was an exhilarating but terrifying feeling.'

Radhika was finally free. For the first time in a very long time she felt that she and Rohan might have a chance of a decent future with someone like Jigmi.

Jigmi's one-bedroom apartment was only a brisk, 20-minute walk from the centre of Sonagachi. It was on the third floor of a five-storey building and notable for its absence of anything personal. There wasn't a single photograph anywhere or any of the personal objects that usually give a clue to a person's character. Despite this it was homely enough, with a few smart carpets and a nice sofa and dining room table and chairs, although the white walls gave it a slightly clinical air, Radhika felt. The flat suggested its tenant did little else in life other than work and sleep. Still, it was a million times better than the brothel.

Once safely inside his apartment, Jigmi told Radhika to make herself at home on the sofa, while he caught up with some sleep ready for work the next day. Once again, he kissed Radhika chastely on the forehead and said goodnight to her before retiring to a separate bed. She was so weary that she instantly fell asleep, knowing that – for the moment at least – she was safe.

When Radhika awoke the next morning, Jigmi had already left and she found herself slowly relaxing for the first time in many months. Rohan never slipped out of Radhika's mind for more than a few seconds and huge waves of guilt broke through the brief moments of happiness she was able to feel at being free of the brothel. But the pressures of working there were beginning to take their toll and she was concerned that she might not have the strength to make it back to Kathmandu if she did realize her dream quickly and rescue Rohan. She knew that she had to rest while she had the chance. Who knew what lay ahead after all?

Taking Jigmi at his word to make herself at home, she took a long soak in his clean white bath, scrubbing the dirt and the squalor of the last few months off her body, trying to make herself clean again.

Examining the smooth contours of her slim figure, she saw the evidence of her forced trade on her body. Once, her pale olive skin had been flawless, now it bore the scars of human trafficking. Most prominent was the ugly tear that ran defiantly along her left side. It was a constant reminder of the terrible episode in Chennai that had resulted in her kidney being stolen from her. To Radhika, it was a symbol of her naivety and sheer powerlessness. And now cigarette burns and a disfigured patch of skin near her right shin, caused by a kick from a drunken client were testament to her gallery of pain and degradation. She sought solace in something one of her fellow prostitutes had once told her. 'Scars are beautiful. They are proof that you are a survivor.' And that much was true. Radhika was certainly proving herself to be a survivor along with her son, Rohan. Now all she had to do was find him and get away from the city as quickly as possible.

Jigmi returned home from work at around 5 p.m. that first evening, bearing a bag filled with cooked rice, dhal and naan bread bought from the market. He confessed to Radhika that he had never learned to cook and lived on takeaways. Radhika, who still barely knew him, was touched by his kindness. She was also impatient as she was anxious for them to make a plan to get Rohan back.

'I was terrified I would be recaptured by Tamang before long and I felt guilty for indulging in [such] luxury while Rohan was imprisoned somewhere terrible. Whatever it took, I had to find him – fast.

'Jigmi said he had started to make subtle enquiries in and around Sonagachi about Rohan's whereabouts and had a couple of leads that he promised to follow up. He told me I should relax and regain some strength. At that moment, our eyes locked.'

Well aware of what men wanted, Radhika knew that Jigmi desired her. 'I allowed him to pull me gently towards him and he began gently kissing my forehead before moving to my neck and down towards my breasts. I had never been touched by anyone like that before and it felt electrifying.'

But despite the chemistry between them and Radhika's gratitude for what he had done for her, Jigmi never demanded full sexual intercourse, a fact that some might find baffling. Radhika, however, is still grateful to him for his warmth and consideration at a time when she was at her most vulnerable. He did not demand payment for his help, even though she would willingly have given it to him.

She comments, 'Jigmi did not go further but I didn't feel rejected in any way because he had made me feel so special. I'm not sure why he stopped but he didn't seem to need sexual intercourse to feel fulfilled. I'm sure he had his own reasons but we never spoke about it. It just felt wonderful to be touched as a woman rather than mauled or pawed like an animal.'

For Radhika, who had been forced to have sex with up to 30 men a day, this treatment was extraordinary.

For the next six days Radhika lived in Jigmi's apartment under the guise of his girlfriend. Jigmi's routine was quite rigid: each day he would go to work and each night, he would bring home fresh food for them to eat, before snuggling up next to Radhika on the sofa. She could almost believe the pretence was true, but at the forefront of her mind was Rohan. Where he was. What he was doing. If he was missing. If he had been punished for her escape.

Each night, Jigmi would report back to Radhika about his progress in scouring different parts of the city for Rohan. But it was taking too long for Radhika, who was torn between an overwhelming feeling of gratitude to Jigmi and the torment that the forced separation from her son was bringing. She was also aware that the longer she stayed in the city, the more likely it was that she might be recaptured. Who knew what the Tamangs would do to her if they discovered her with Jigmi? She already knew what Maya Tamang was capable of. Aware that such thoughts were getting her nowhere, she forced herself to stop thinking so negatively. Of course, it was going to work. It just had to. She had to escape.

On the seventh day of freedom, a soft knock on the door changed everything. Convinced it must be Jigmi returning home from work early, Radhika answered the door without first checking who it was, something that Jigmi had ordered her to do for her own safety. As the door swung open she realized her mistake. There, in front of her were three of Maya Tamang's most frightening men. She tried to slam the door shut but it was too late. They forced it open, grabbing her roughly by the arms as one of them screamed into the terrified girl's face: '*Come with us you fucking whore! It's time to go back to hell!*'

Shaking with fear, Radhika had no choice but to give in, listening helplessly as they jostled and manhandled her, whispering abuse and dire warnings of what would happen to her at the brothel. On the way back to the brothel, she spared a brief moment's thought for Jigmi and what might happen to him. She prayed that he would be kept safe, that he might receive some warning of what had happened. The alternative was simply unthinkable. And she had Rohan to worry about and what punishment Maya Tamang might mete out when she returned to the brothel. She had to concentrate on that. She must keep herself alive no matter what – Rohan's life depended on it.

She was dragged back over the threshold of the brothel, struggling all the way. She knew it was useless to do so but she couldn't help herself. When she'd left the house with Jigmi, anything had seemed possible, now her dreams lay shattered before her.

Maya Tamang stood waiting. She studied the struggling girl for a moment, her face expressionless, before spitting straight into her face. She shrieked, 'You have humiliated and deceived me, you good-for-nothing bitch. *Now* you will feel pain like you have never felt before.'

With these words, her temper was fully unleashed. Radhika knew that everything she had suffered at this woman's hands in the past was nothing compared to what would happen to her now. She flinched, cowering as Maya Tamang proceeded to slap the right side of her face, so hard that she drew blood from her ear.

Her head ringing with pain, Radhika watched helplessly as the brothel owner extracted a long piece of lead piping from behind a chair, swinging it in a menacing fashion as her eyes locked with Radhika's. The men who had brought her back to the brothel stood still, watching to see what would happen next. Almost in slow motion, Maya Tamang swung the pipe up high, paused for one second and then brought it down with all her might on Radhika's head. She felt a flash of pain, more intense than she had ever felt before, had a moment to wonder if she was dead, and then – nothing.

A heavy metallic smell filled her nostrils when she finally awoke more than hour later. She tried to place it, but she couldn't. She felt too ill. Then the pain hit and she remembered what had happened. Realized that the smell was that of her own blood. Forcing her eyes open, Radhika blinked rapidly, trying to focus on her surroundings, but all she could see was black. For a moment she panicked. Was she blind? Had Maya Tamang's blow affected her sight? She forced herself to breathe more slowly, burying the panic. When she eventually came back to proper consciousness she realized just where she was.

She had heard about 'the dungeon' from the other girls at the brothel who had been put in there by the brothel owner for alleged misdeeds or just because she felt like it.

A separate chamber in the building, it was a cellar-like structure, covered by a small trap door. Inside, it was pitch black and a rat, the sound of which Radhika could hear scratching on the sodden floor beneath her, ran around, foraging for something tasty to nibble on.

Apart from that creature, it was eerily quiet. Radhika called out, her voice hoarse, almost unrecognizable initially. But after a while, her yells became louder, stronger. Still no one came. She wondered if the girls had been told to ignore her – or if, unlike her, they just knew better than to acknowledge her, fearful of what Maya Tamang might do to them if they did. Still she yelled; still she shouted; occasionally she screamed. Sometimes she was just silent. She did this for two days and two nights. For most of them, she sat slumped with her back against a wall without food and water, forced to defecate and urinate in the small room. How had her life come to this? Could she physically and mentally cope with any more before shutting down completely?

Even though Radhika felt broken in mind and body, once again she managed to summon up the strength from somewhere to survive. She had to be ok. Who would look after Rohan otherwise? A tiny spark of hope remained that

Jigmi might still be alive and had rescued Rohan, but the more time she spent in the dungeon, the less likely this seemed. If she ever got out of here, if the gods allowed her to live, *she* would have to rescue her son. Rohan was her only reason for staying alive. He was her life. Without him she was nothing. Maya Tamang might do everything in her power to destroy Radhika but she would never break her promise to her son. No matter what, she would somehow stay alive for him.

And so, when the trap door finally opened and she emerged from hell into the light, leaving the horrific confines of Maya Tamang's torture chamber behind her, she knew that she would have to bide her time until she could get to Rohan. She knew she would have to go back to selling her body to strangers, until another moment arose when she could escape with Rohan. She knew all this and accepted it as her fate.

As she washed away the dried blood, urine and faeces caked to her body and soothed her aching bruises, Radhika emerged stronger, clearer headed and even more determined than before that *this* would not be her life forever.

Bollywood dreams

ROHAN screamed. The sound was so harrowing that it seemed to pierce Radhika's heart.

She hadn't been informed of a visit from her beloved son and knew that his presence at the brothel could only signal one thing – that they were about to be moved again. It was hardly surprising given her attempted escape with Jigmi.

Jigmi – she tried hard not to think of him.

Rohan was now two-and-a-half years old and was displaying the signs of a severe attachment disorder. He had not been allowed to bond with his mother in the crucial stages of early development and as a result he was now often angry or withdrawn. The effects were hardly surprising considering he had been wrenched from Radhika by the sex traffickers when he was just over a year old and had been held captive in a series of horrific compounds while she was forced to prostitute herself.

Along with the children of other prostitutes, a panic-stricken Rohan was often left alone for hours on end and any signs of his distress were met with cold indifference, at best, and violence, at worst.

Rohan's suffering was the hardest cross for Radhika to bear. Brothel owners could beat her within an inch of her life but they could never come close to inflicting the kind of pain she felt knowing she was failing her tiny son. He had already been trafficked to two brothels and Radhika's contact with Rohan had been limited to just 3 visits, each lasting 15 minutes at most, in the past 6 months.

Rohan's cries intensified as he was dragged roughly along the corridor towards his mother's room in the Sonagachi brothel. Radhika quickly clambered out of the bath in which she had been attempting to wash away the bloody residue of her most recent beating, donning a loose white cotton kurta to cover her bruises, before going to find her son.

She immediately ran towards Rohan and gathered him up in her arms, ignoring her own pain as she smothered his reddened, tear-stained face with kisses. He didn't react to her, but by now she was used to his detachment from her. She could see Rohan was deeply distressed. Worse still, he was in terrible and obvious pain.

'I began trying to soothe Rohan by feeding him some biscuits and milk,' she recalls. 'It was then that I noticed the terrible wound in his mouth. I shouted at the woman who had accompanied him to the brothel and demanded to know what had happened to my son. She didn't even try to lie or cover up the truth. She looked at me coldly and said: "He was crying too much so we burned his mouth with a cigarette. It taught him a lesson."'

For a moment, Radhika was utterly speechless, staring incredulously at the monster in front of her. Then she let out a heart-wrenching scream, before breaking down into uncontrollable sobs.

What kind of evil people would do such a thing? To hurt such a helpless little boy in such a horrific way. And what kind of a mother was she to let such terrible things happen to her child? No wonder Rohan seemed to treat her with such coldness. Who could blame him? She had let him down. She couldn't even protect him properly. In that moment, she knew that she had to find some way of getting them out of this situation as soon as she possibly could.

Radhika drew in several deep breaths, making an effort to pull herself together. She had to stay calm for Rohan's sake. He was living in a world of chaos and the last thing he needed was his own mother adding to his distress.

Turning away from the woman, who was watching her distress with such dispassion, Radhika went to her room. She found her spare black kurta and soaked it in cold water, making a compress which she then attempted to lay gently against Rohan's mouth.

She tried not to let her own pain show in her face. She could see that Rohan's wound was raw and infected. He screamed as she laid the material against the wound. His harrowing cries felt like daggers in Radhika's heart.

'I felt completely broken. Rohan just screamed and screamed until he eventually sobbed himself to sleep.

'I rock[ed] him back and forth on my knee when Maya Tamang stormed in[to the room] and told me: "You are … worthless to me. Pack your bags you traitor[ous] bitch and get ready to go to Delhi."

'Even if she had told me I was going to hell [at that point], I think I would have felt better. Anywhere had to be better than the evil regime she ran in the stinking slums of Kolkata.'

Tamang introduced Radhika to a woman who she claimed was her sister, but Radhika didn't catch her name. She was told that this woman was to be her chaperone and would acccompany Radhika on the 1,305km (811 mile) train journey from Kolkata to New Delhi, her next destination.

At this point, as Radhika tried to cope with her screaming son, she wasn't quite sure if it mattered where they ended up.

They began the familiar, arduous trek from Bengal to the capital, first by train and then by bus. Almost immune to her surroundings, Radhika stared blankly at the beautiful scenery that sped by as the train made its way across the vast continent.

At first, when she had been forced to make these journeys, the beauty of India, the diversity of its landscape, the differences between it and her native country had all struck her, making her feel somehow insignificant. Now, these trips were just synonymous with her and Rohan's continued suffering and she could barely bring herself to look at the landscape. It didn't really matter where she and Rohan were sent to, she never got a chance to view the cities, to witness their magnificence first-hand. Radhika only saw the underbelly of society – humanity at its very worst.

Radhika's primary concern was her son. Rohan's infected wound had caused him to develop a worryingly high temperature and she was terrified.

She hadn't spent much time with her son in over a year and she hadn't been a proper mother to him in that time. She quite simply had never seen him this ill before. Now, she worried that he might not survive; after all they had gone through and the promises that she hadn't been able to keep to him, Radhika simply couldn't bear it.

'I had always been concerned about staying alive for Rohan's sake, but it had never occurred to me that his life might actually become endangered too. I sat watching his every breath as he drifted in and out of sleep.

'I was afraid that his heart might suddenly miss a beat. For me life was a simple equation – without Rohan it was nothing. If he [died], I would take my life.'

This time the gods were with them. Towards the end of the two-day journey Rohan began to show signs of recovery. Radhika had begged a fellow passenger for paracetemol tablets and they had at least eased the little boy's pain, even though he was still desperately in need of antibiotics.

They arrived in New Delhi one evening in September 2006. Time was no longer important to Radhika. All she could focus on was their day-to-day survival. Foremost on her mind was that while Rohan had got through this particular ordeal, what if he didn't next time?

Her first glimpse of the city made it pretty much indistinguishable from any other that Radhika had lived in since coming to India.

Sightseeing was not part of a prostitute's world so there would be no opportunities to marvel at the beauty of the Red Fort or take in the Lodi Gardens. During her time in the country, she hadn't been allowed to do the usual things that one might do with a young child in a new place: Radhika's world had been confined to the red-light districts in which she worked.

As before, she was taken, this time by taxi, to yet another area of depravity, where she was to resume her duties as a prostitute. Yet again, she was to be separated from Rohan, and that she dreaded more than anything else.

GB (Garstin Bastion) Road is an infamous red-light district in the heart of India's capital, made up of around 20 buildings housing a brothel, usually located on the first and second floors. Just 10 minutes from where the bus had dropped them off, it is an area in which hundreds of young girls live as virtual prisoners in unspeakable squalor. Some are born into prostitution and resign themselves after years of observing their mothers performing sexual favours to follow the same path. Others, like Radhika, have been dragged into this underworld through lies and deception. Many, like Radhika, are of Nepalese origin*. Once again, Radhika wrapped Rohan in a thick scarf and strapped him onto her back as she walked into the four-storey building with a heavy heart, past the shops that made up part of Asia's largest hardware market.

The brothel was located on the first floor, the steep stone steps leading up to the Kothas (or rooms) of the sexworkers. At the entrance, Radhika glimpsed a painted sign warning customers to beware of pickpockets, but she knew from experience that it was usually the pimps and Madames themselves who doubled up as thieves.

Four or five older girls greeted Radhika in the passageway. They seemed friendly enough. One of them barked at her in a husky smoker's voice. 'The boss is coming. She's been waiting for you.'

At that moment, a lean, middle-aged Indian woman with fair skin came striding towards Radhika. Her tight-fitting yellow sari was stained with cooking oil and her white, plastic, high-heeled sandals revealed gnarled toes with chipped red nail polish. She immediately began reeling off

*According to Dr Govinda Prasad Kusum, Nepal's Secretary for Ministry of Home Affairs, between 7 and 10,000 girls are being trafficked to India every month.

the house rules to Radhika but they seemed no different to those of the other places that she had been forced to live in. Her mind began to wander.

'For the first time, I really felt like I had hit rock bottom. I had a feeling that I would never attain freedom. After all the pain and suffering, I was convinced that Rohan and I would have to spend the rest of our lives this way.'

Her thoughts were interrupted by the Madame who was trying to remove Rohan from his mother's back. She didn't want her son to become even more distressed so Radhika untied him herself, asking if she could have a few moments alone with him before they took him away from her. To her great surprise, the Madame agreed.

'I sat on the steps of the brothel smoothing his forehead and singing his favourite "Twinkle Twinkle" nursery rhyme.

'"Please believe me, Rohan," I whispered to him. "This time it won't be for long. Somehow I will find a way of giving you a better life."

'I planted kisses on his face before quickly handing him over. This time it had to be fast. Even though we had been through this kind of separation before, it wasn't getting any easier. [B]y now I knew that it was futile to ask where Rohan was going. Keeping his whereabouts a secret was key to keeping me in the brothel.'

To Radhika's great distress, Rohan did not let out a single sound when he left her. That cut through Radhika like a knife, but she forced herself to remain silent as she watched her son being carried away, even though she was not at all sure when she would next set eyes on him. Rohan seemed more comfortable with strangers than with his own mother – and that thought made her all the more determined that they would escape this life.

Her heart in her mouth, she tried not to cry as she followed another prostitute to the room allocated for her use. It consisted of the usual prison cell layout. A low bed with a thin, stained mattress and brown blanket was in one corner and a woodworm-infested coffee table stood bleakly in another. Only a small wooden window with rotting shutters provided an outlet for the pungent stench of sweat and sex. From the balcony, she glimpsed the Holiday Inn hotel and across the road lay the Indian Railways Coach Care Centre from which tourists tried to take photos of her and the other girls. At such times, she felt like an animal in a zoo.

At least, she thought, she appeared to have a room to herself this time. The room's roughly plastered walls were also alleviated from complete squalor by the Bollywood posters featuring some of her favourite heroes. There, locked in dreamy dance poses were actors Salman Khan, Sanjay Dutt, Hrithik Roshan and Rani Mukerji. They stared down at Radhika, lifting her spirits briefly – beauty in an otherwise ugly environment.

'You like Bollywood, huh?', said an older prostitute, laughing as she noticed Radhika's interest in the film posters. 'Just as well.... You'll have to adopt an actress's name for the customers. It's the rule [here].'

She turned abruptly away and ran barefoot down the rickety stairs, leaving Radhika alone to slump down onto the bed, where she continued to gaze up at the posters.

'I knew immediately that I was going to be Rinke after Rinke Khanna. I had always admired her sultry beauty and ... it would be easier to get through the long days and nights pretending to be someone else.'

Radhika had been captivated by Bollywood from a young age. She mainly had to rely on magazines and old newspapers to devour the gossip about the exotic films and their glamorous stars. But on one memorable occasion, as a 12-year-old girl, Radhika's cousin had taken her and her sisters to the Balaju Cinema Hall in Nepal for a screening of *Seema Rekha*. A Nepalese movie that raises questions about the country's unification, it draws on Bollywood, featuring a series of well-choreographed music and dance routines.

'I remember sitting there spellbound as the music and dancing began and the story started to unfold,' she recalls. '*Seema Rekha* means 'border line' in Nepali. It's incredible to think how significant that was later on. How could I ever have imagined just how many times I would be forced to cross borders myself in later years or the torment I would suffer in doing so.

'I developed a passion for Bollywood, which at times bordered on an obsession. My favourite actors are Salman Khan, Rani Mukerji and Shahid Kapoor. All of them are known for their unique dancing styles. Salman Khan represents a typical macho man character whereas Shahid Kapoor is known for his romantic lead roles.

'My favourite movies are those where there is a lot of action and where heroes fight with millions of villains to get their love back. My role [in real life] was to get Rohan back, but first I knew I would have [to be a prostitute] once again.'

GB Road's clientele was not dissimilar to that of the previous brothels where Radhika had worked. There were the usual middle-aged customers in the form of low-paid office workers and labourers, supplemented by a mix of students and soldiers, all of whom staggered in late at night for a fix of the house liquor before hitting the 'catwalk' and taking a gamble with their health and lives. While Radhika was still disease free, she was becoming adept at recognizing the symptoms of HIV/AIDS in others, such as weight loss, a lack of energy, skin and nail infections and deep chesty coughs. Looking around, she guessed that many of the other girls in this brothel had been struck by the disease.

The routine in each brothel was pretty much the same – stand on the 'catwalk' and wait to be picked before leading the client to the room and clinically stripping down to a lace negligee and knickers or some other lingerie. In New Delhi, she was given two sets of underwear – one lime green and the other cerise pink. The nylon material was cheap and it made her skin itch. After being chosen, Radhika's routine would be to sink down as seductively as she could onto the thin mattress and wait for her client to thrust himself into her. It often felt uncomfortable, sometimes it felt excruciating and it was always humiliating. Radhika would stare fixedly at the wall, transporting herself out of the squalor and into a Bollywood dream instead as each pair of flabby, hairy male buttocks bumped up and down on top of her. Radhika was gone, but her other persona, Rinke, remained. She was off in a world full of Bollywood plots featuring at least one set of star-crossed lovers and a happy-ever-after ending.

Anything, it seemed, was achievable in Bollywood and thinking of the plots of some of these films gave Radhika hope when she felt down about Rohan. The separation from him was getting harder to bear, particularly after the terrible abuse he had suffered in Kolkata. Her mind was full of questions: Who was caring for him now? Was he still sick? What kind of squalor was he living in?

Radhika could not count the times she had felt she would be better off dead – but that would be the selfish way out. How could she leave Rohan alone? Her family had no idea where they were, or even if they were alive. She had no option but to carry on.

There was only one person she could rely on – herself – and so Radhika began to think and scheme in earnest, planning ways to escape from the brothel and this life. Her main problem was the brothel owners themselves. They were smart and streetwise and also obviously talked to each other; her attempted escape with Jigmi must have made her current captors even more wary of her. Befriending the brothel owner was out of the question – all she cared about was counting her rupees at the end of each day. Human life was superfluous to the real business of making money and, of course, the woman knew that with Rohan squirrelled away, Radhika would do anything to keep him safe.

After six months of working in New Delhi, the brothel owner informed Radhika that she was 'refreshing' her staff. Radhika and Rohan were being moved on again. This time, she was being sent to a brothel in Pune, the eighth largest city in India, and the second largest in the state of Maharashtra, after Mumbai.

Rohan and Radhika were reunited for the first time in months. Radhika felt the tears prick when she saw how his tiny features had changed in the months since they had last last seen each other. She checked him over carefully, terrified that her son might have been further abused. This time there were no external injuries, at least – no bruises, tears or cuts and no evidence of cigarettes cruelly extinguished on his young flesh. But Radhika could see the fear and horror in his eyes and his sadness was an almost tangible force. The psychological damage that her son had suffered was something that she couldn't measure. Rohan's inability to communicate made it difficult to judge how badly he had been affected by the months of separation and abuse. All she could do was pray that one day their luck would change and she would be able to get Rohan the help that he deserved.

After being bundled into a rickshaw by their chaperone, the group made the long 48-hour journey across the 1,417km (880 miles) from New Delhi to the Budhwar Peth district of Pune. By the time they arrived, Radhika and Rohan were both exhausted. On the journey, Radhika had relished spending time with her son. He seemed to relax after a while. She still wasn't sure if he recognized her; the months that they had spent apart now more than their time together, but he seemed healthier than the last time she had seen him and the appalling injury to his mouth seemed to have healed, although only the gods knew the psychological scars caused by such abuse. Rohan still didn't speak and he also didn't appear to recognize things from their past, such as his favourite nursery rhymes. Radhika still sang them to him on the journey, appearing to all intents and purposes to their fellow passengers, a normal, loving mother tending to her child. Inside, she felt differently, however. She had to take a stand. And soon.

She decided to fight to keep Rohan with her from now on. In New Delhi, Rohan had been lucky – if 'luck' was the right word to use – because he seemingly hadn't been mistreated. But how could she guarantee he would receive similar treatment in Pune? Or the next place? Or the one after that? Still young and attractive enough, Radhika was aware she had years in her yet in which to earn her traffickers a fortune. If she didn't act to stop them first.

She glanced around, aware for the first time of her strange surroundings. 'I had no concept at all of where we were. I had given up asking because my questions were always met with the same indifferen[ce, the same] arrogant silences. The owner of the brothel [this time] was a woman called Saili. There was a glimmer of softness in her eyes, which told me that I might have some bargaining power with Rohan.

'This time I stood firm and told her that she could not take my son. I vowed to sleep with as many clients as she wished, but I said I would kill myself rather than be separated from Rohan again.

'She looked at me for a moment and then said: "So be it. But what will you do with him when you are entertaining clients?" Radhika told the woman that she would persuade the other girls in the brothel to look after him. She was determined that Rohan would remain with her. Then, when she was asleep, for the first time in months, her child would be by her side. Nothing would prevent that.

Saili was reluctant to give in but the months of working in India's toughest brothels had hardened Radhika. On this she would not budge. She was also aware that Saili was slightly different to the Tamangs, softer and therefore perhaps more lenient. Determined to play this to her advantage, Radhika began to cry. She screamed, ranted and raved, anything to convince this woman that she could not, would not be separated from her son. In the end, Saili relented. Radhika had won. For the first time, in a very long time, she had some semblance of control over her life, over the *most* important part of her life – she and her son would stay together. For Radhika this was one essential battle won – and one step closer to freedom.

Radhika settled in quickly, making alliances with the other girls, aware that Rohan's very happiness, very well-being depended on these relationships.

Some girls were extremely kind, occupying the young boy by playing simple clapping games with him or entertaining him with nursery rhymes while Radhika worked. They usually had children themselves or little brothers and sisters who they missed. Rohan, by his presence, through his very innocence, gave them a glimpse of their former lives. But when they had clients Rohan would have to remain in Radhika's small windowless section of a four-bed dormitory, while his own mother had sex with strangers.

She tried to shield Rohan, as much as she could, from the sordid reality of their situation, concocting elaborate stories about the men being unwell. She told Rohan that she was just acting like a nurse and that they needed hugs from her to get better, but she knew deep down that their grunts and groans and the stench of stale liquor belied her story.

Knowing she had no choice and that separation would be worse for both of them, she struggled to protect Rohan as best she could. She made it clear to him that he had to lie perfectly still at all times when he was told to hide beneath the bed. And although Radhika felt like she was failing her son on every level, she simply could not risk him being sent away to suffer more abuse at some stranger's hands.

The fact that she had placed her son in a situation where he could hear her having sex with strangers, some of whom were less than gentle, sometimes even violent, drove Radhika to desperately scheme and plan for their escape. She was always on her guard, ever watchful for a chance to grab him and run. But the opportunity did not arise during their time in Pune.

In the end, Radhika and Rohan stayed together for three months before Saili called her into her room. She introduced Radhika to a fat, middle-aged woman, her chaperone on the 180km (111 mile) bus journey to Mumbai, Bollywood capital and the heart of India's sex trade, where she would work in a brothel located in the infamous red-light district of Kamathipura.

Clutching her dreams to her chest, Radhika accompanied Rohan on the next stage of their journey, praying to Lakshmi and Lord Ganesh that this time it might lead to escape.

By now Radhika was all too familiar with the sights and smells of India's red-light districts, but Kamathipura proved even more overwhelming than the other places she had been forced to work in right from the outset because of the extent of the depravity existing there. Originally established by the British Raj in the 19th century for their troops, the district has since become the largest red-light district in the world and it was here Radhika had been sent to work.

Radhika swung Rohan onto her back, making sure he was securely bound to her. They scurried along behind the chaperone after disembarking from the bus, walking as quickly as they could through the meandering unfamiliar streets. The place was a maze and they walked quite some distance, well over 3km (1.8 miles) through the depressing high-rise buildings, most in a poor standard of condition, with their paint peeling and rotting wood beneath.

Women lolled about in the crowded streets, lounging in the broken doorways of nearby buildings, leaning provocatively against dirty street walls, jostling each other out of the way as they competed for business. As Radhika and Rohan passed them by, some screamed obscenities at them. Others whispered or shouted about the acts they could perform, the 'dreams' they could fulfil. One thing was clear from the outset to Radhika, as she tried to shield her son as best she could from the scenes around them: every perversion or vile sexual act a man could dream of was here in this little world for the taking if the price was right.

For Radhika even by the standards of the other sex areas she had been in, this was a veritable hell. She glanced at the children playing and crawling in the overflowing gutters spewing sewage, rubbish, rotting food and god knows what else onto the streets. Rats darted in and out of the shadows and cockroaches scurried around. As she glanced around, she spied one boy of about Rohan's age, dirty, malnourished and poorly dressed. She blinked back the tears. There was absolutely no way Rohan would end up like this. She simply wouldn't let it happen.

Finally, after what seemed an age, their companion stopped outside a four-storey corner building. She greeted the brothel owner. Before Radhika could even speak up, she was amazed to hear her chaperone tell the woman that a deal had already been struck and that Rohan was to stay with his mother. Radhika was pleased that she had been right about Saili, the Pune brothel Madame, who had allowed Rohan to stay with her.

She sighed as the new Madame beckoned her inside the dark building. She was a grossly overweight Indian woman in her mid-40s. Her bright pink sari exposed her protruding belly, which sagged in endless rolls above her petticoats. Radhika was led upstairs to a small room, where she met her new roommates.

Her first thought was pity for the three girls who were introduced to her. They were even younger than she was, about the age she had been when had taken that first fateful sip of Coca–Cola, she thought. They were also Nepalese. They reminded her of herself years ago. She couldn't suppress the heartache she felt as she looked at them.

Each of the girls was slim and petite, the tallest slightly smaller than Radhika, at around 1.58m (5ft 2ins). Riya and Reeta were both 17, while Laxmi was the baby at 16. Radhika could see they still had life left in them; she was relieved that unlike so many of the girls that she had met over the last few months they still had some spirit, some dignity, left. They all took pride in their appearances, maintaining some semblance of style, despite the dinginess of their surroundings.

Reeta had highlighted dark hair, which was carefully woven into a stylish plait. Riya and Laxmi's black locks were glossy and lovingly brushed back into a neat ponytail. Dressed in brightly coloured saris, they wore them with style and grace. Still, despite their bravado, Radhika could see that they had all endured terrible experiences in this horrific environment. They, too, had been trafficked from Nepal after being lured to India with the promise of better jobs in grocery stores and carpet factories. But they were clearly making the best of a bad situation and Radhika admired them for that.

The girls instantly took to one another. They fussed over Rohan and promised Radhika that they would take care of the young boy. They were true to their word and over the next weeks, they went to great lengths to shield the little boy from the kind of sights that no child should ever have to bear witness to.

As Radhika tried to calm her mind and surrender to sleep each night, she would question whether her decision to bring Rohan into the brothel had been the right one. While it was true that at least here she could protect him from physical harm, on the other hand, how could she tell what untold damage the experience was doing to him emotionally?

She worried about this night after night, aware that her son was already so traumatized by his experiences. The image of that boy playing in the sewers embedded in her mind, she promised herself that she would get them away from this world soon, before Rohan was much older.

But the question was now 'How?'

THE RETURN
OF
HOPE

The
great escape

STARS shone brightly across Mumbai during one of the coldest winter nights in living memory.

Inside the freezing brothel, Radhika, Laxmi, Riya and Reeta drew the curtains around their filthy third-floor cubicle and huddled together in a tight circle; eyes wide, they clutched desperately at each other's hands. The four girls had plotted how to escape and the time had come for their plan to be executed.

The girls' terror was palpable; all of them were aware that if even one thing went wrong they were doomed. They began to recount their plans, going through them meticulously in detail even though they had done so more times than any of them could recall. Now tired, emotional, terrified yet also excited, they went methodically through their escape plan one last time, each aware that if one of them made even a tiny error, all of their lives – including that of little Rohan's – would be over. The stakes were just too high for them to mess up at this late stage in the game.

At just 16 years of age, Reeta was the self-styled ringleader of their little gang. With pale skin and chiselled features, she possessed the kind of beauty that would have, in another lifetime and with a few more inches added to her height, arguably have catapulted her to great success as a model or actress. But what she lacked in height she made up for in character. Reeta was feisty, direct and honest. She was a planner; she never left anything to chance. She was unfailingly positive in her attitude, making the best of her lot but also totally unwilling to accept the label of 'victim'. She simply did not accept that she was going to be a prostitute for the rest of her life. So, she schemed and planned and chivvied the rest of them on, until they had tonight's plan in place. Until they believed escape was possible.

Reeta was reluctant to discuss her upbringing, perhaps indicating that it had been harsh and she didn't really want to dwell on it. But it was clear from the start that she and the other girls hailed from Nepal, something that had immediately drawn them all together. Reeta was also a natural leader and gave out orders with almost military precision. In another time, another place, she could potentially have done more with her life, as even at the tender age of 16, people listened to Reeta when she spoke.

'Remember, the most important thing is to stay calm,' she whispered to her comrades. 'We will leave in 10 minutes at approximately 2 a.m. and make our way downstairs together.

'I will lead the way and stay out in front. Radhika, Rohan and Riya will be in the middle and Laxmi will lag a little way behind. If the security guards at the back of the building are still absent, we will walk confidently out of the door. If they have returned, you will hear me say: "Namaste" and that will be your signal to go back to the room. Then I will simply say that I am thirsty and have come to get [some] water.

'If everything goes to plan and we … make it [out of] the door, we will walk quickly to the station [and] Riya, Laxmi and I will go ahead of Radhika and Rohan to buy tickets for us all.

'Now this bit is important,' she paused, studying her friends' faces intently, before saying with great emphasis, *DO... NOT... RUN!* [We do not want to alert] anyone.'

Reeta looked at her friends intently, girls that had come to mean so much to her within such a very short space of time, and on whom she was staking her future. She scanned their faces, reading the same fear that she tried to bury deep inside herself. When she spoke again, her voice was shaking and tears pricked at her eyes:

'Now, find all the courage you can and go [fight] for your lives. Remember, whatever happens to us from now on can be no worse than what we have to endure here each day.

'We have nothing to lose other than our lives – and what is life worth here?'

All the girls nodded. All of them felt the same as Reeta. This close-knit group of girls was about to risk everything in a daring bid for freedom. But even if their plan failed, there were few worse punishments that could be meted out than being forced to sleep with up to 30 clients a day, that they all knew. The risk for them was worth it.

In the weeks leading up to this day, Reeta, Riya and Laxmi, had helped Radhika and Rohan to settle in as best they could. Within a very short time, she became close to them, partly because they lavished such care and attention on Rohan.

Radhika had told her new friends everything about her previous experiences, particularly confiding how Rohan had suffered at the hands of the brothel owners. He was still disturbingly subdued and remained worryingly unattached to his mother, something that broke her heart. But, with the help of the girls, who did everything possible to help out, Radhika was able to protect him from further abuse in Mumbai. Her friends took turns to cuddle Rohan, singing to him, feeding him and even stroking his hair until he slept, almost as if he were their own.

The girls confided in their new friend that they had been planning to escape ever since December 2006, when they had first arrived at the brothel in Mumbai and finally realized that far from getting lucrative jobs, they were to be sold as prostitutes to anyone willing to pay the cheap price.

They refused to let their spirits be broken by the relentless misery of their day-to-day existence and instead remained defiant, unwilling to accept that their lot was a life in captivity. With Reeta in the driving seat, they plotted and schemed to find a way out of the brothel.

Knowing money was essential to any successful plot and learning quickly that anything they earned immediately went to the brothel owner, they came up with a somewhat risky plan to extort money from their own clients.

Most of the men turned up at the house after work and quickly became inebriated on the cheap booze that the brothel owner sold to them, before they even got to choose their girl or girls from the catwalk. Most were barely able to stand by the time they got to that stage. At great risk to themselves, the girls began to take money from the pockets of their most intoxicated clients, stashing it under a loose floorboard next to Reeta's bed.

By the time Radhika and Rohan arrived in the city, the girls had extracted enough money not only to fund their own escapes but that of their new friend and her young son's as well. Their kindness to Radhika and Rohan in including them in their plans was beyond expression. Radhika, who had gone through the trauma of her unsuccessful escape with Jigmi, already understood the risks involved. She still hoped that Jigmi was alive, but knew in her heart that this was unlikely. But she had reached breaking point. She couldn't take it any more and she didn't want Rohan to be exposed to the depraved and debauched reality of brothel life any longer. While Reeta, Riya and Laxmi made life much easier for them, at any point Radhika was aware that her life could change radically and that she could be forced to move to another brothel, where Rohan might be wrenched from her arms again. She couldn't stand that thought. She had to take the chance that Reeta's plan might actually work.

Radhika looked at her friends as they whispered their thoughts, plans, hopes and dreams to each other in the darkness. Their confidence was infectious. This time the plan *would* work. There was simply no way it could not.

Lady Lakshmi seemed to be with them the night of the escape. For some reason, the security guards had stopped manning the doors at night, most probably to save the Madame money. They had chosen 2 a.m. as the hour for their escape as it always coincided with a lull in the night's events. At that point, most of the usual customers had already staggered home and any overnight guests were either fast asleep or otherwise engaged in getting their money's worth from their chosen girl.

With a strong feeling of déjà vu, Radhika once again packed her belongings into a small carrier bag. She had gone through this ritual before but hoped this time would be the last. By now, she owned just two tired looking kurtas and a bottle of half empty shampoo. She peeled off her prostitute uniform (a tight, short black Lycra skirt and yellow basque top) and threw them contemptuously onto the floor. Pulling on a plain black kurta tunic and some ripped blue jeans and slipping into a pair of black slippers, Radhika felt like she was shedding a layer of skin to reveal her old and true self. She prayed to the gods that she would never have to wear her 'prostitute' clothes again.

Reeta signalled that the old alarm clock sitting on the bedside table had hit 2 a.m. and that it was time to go. Radhika's breath quickened as she tied Rohan to her back with a stained, blue pashmina and left the room to go to the first floor. The terrible trauma that her son had suffered at the hands of human traffickers had manifested itself into his inability to communicate verbally. Rohan still didn't speak but that didn't prevent Radhika from whispering to him gently, 'Stay as quiet as you can and hang on to Mummy tightly.'

Craning her neck back to smother his face with kisses, Radhika added: 'I know you feel afraid but I promise you, Rohan, I will never let anyone harm you again.

'Try to close your eyes and hopefully when you open them we will be free from this life forever.'

The four girls slowly made their dangerous passage through the brothel. They crept downstairs in absolute terror, worried that the slightest noise might draw unwanted attention to them. Finally, after what seemed hours later they all reached the ground floor. They stole forward, instinct enabling them to find their way through the pitch-black darkness to the back door, where freedom and the outside world beckoned. The building had no lights at the back and the security guards were still absent from their posts. The girls held their breath but it seemed that no one was stirring.

'I could feel my heart beating. We had chosen the perfect night,' Radhika remembers. 'The other girls quickly made their way ahead to the station to buy tickets and Rohan and I were left to hail a rickshaw. At that point I realized I had forgotten to ask Reeta for money to pay the fare but the driver saw the terror on my face and his expression told me he was going to help us. We were on our way.'

The city's street lights flickered past in a blur as Radhika pressed her head back against Rohan's cheek and let the cold night air fill her lungs. Incredibly, Rohan had drifted back into a deep sleep and was oblivious to the tense drama unfolding around him, oblivious to his mother's fears and hopes – fear that everything might go wrong at any second, hope that they might actually succeed.

It seemed like an age before they reached the railway station but in reality the journey took no more than 15 minutes. It was now 2.30 a.m., and although it seemed like hours, just 30 minutes had passed since they had left their rooms in the brothel.

The rickshaw driver smiled reassuringly as he allowed Radhika and Rohan to disembark. Maybe her luck really was changing. Once again she had chanced upon a stranger with good intentions, who didn't seem to expect any kind of pay back. Someone like Jigmi. She quickly buried the thought.

Once inside the railway station, Radhika scanned the interior for her friends. There they were! Laxmi, Riya and Reeta stood at the pre-arranged meeting place. They looked absurdly young, just a typical group of teenage girls waiting for their family to arrive. No one could possibly guess what they had all been through to get to this point; no one could possibly know how great the stakes were for which they were playing.

Radhika walked towards where her friends were gathered in a corner of the ticketing area behind a post. Despite the early hours, there were already a scattering of eager passengers waiting to offload the burden of their luggage onto incoming trains. They hugged briefly and then Reeta thrust a set of tickets into Radhika's hand, along with 500 INR (£7.38). She gathered her close again, all the while careful not to disturb the sleeping Rohan.

'Here sister,' she said, laughing nervously, 'You're [now] halfway home.'

The plan was for Radhika to board a train to Gorakhpur, a city rich in culture and history and one popular with tourists. In the 20th century, the city had been a focal point in the Indian independence movement. It was here that the 'Chauri Chaura' incident took place in February 1922 during British colonial rule. A nationalist mob had set fire to a police station and 23 officers were burned alive inside. Now, Gorakhpur was going to play a big part in the story of Radhika's own struggle for freedom.

A sprawling city and district of over eight million people, Gorakhpur is located in the eastern part of the Indian state of Uttar Pradesh, near the border with Nepal. It is named after the medieval, ascetic saint Gorakshanath, the chief disciple of the yogi Matsyendranath. Together, Matsyendranath and Gorakshanath founded the Nath Sampradaya line of saints. Gorakhnath Temple is said to stand on the spot where Gorakshanath practiced Hatha yoga to develop self-control. And Lord Buddha was born at

Kapilvastu near Gorakhpur, and is thought to have renounced his princely clothing at the confluence of the Rapti and Rohini rivers, before setting out on his quest of truth in around 600 BCE.

If Radhika could make it as far as Gorakhpur, she too could renounce her past life as a prostitute and return home to Nepal and to her family with Rohan, ready to start anew. She had every hope now that her dreams would come true.

The distance from Mumbai to Gorakhpur is approximately 1,631km (1,013 miles) and Radhika and Rohan's train journey was set to last a gruelling three days, making too many stops for Radhika to recall. Once in Gorakhpur, Radhika planned to take a bus to Sunauli, the traditional name given to both sides of this India–Nepal border crossing – 70km (43 miles) north of Gorakhpur and 3km (1.8 miles) south of Bhairahawa. The Indian side is technically Sunauli and the Nepal side is Belahiya. Both are small, congested, dusty and dirty towns.

Meanwhile, Laxmi, Riya and Reeta's planned routes promised to be less taxing. They did not hail from close family units and had no interest in returning home to Nepal. Instead, they had become family for one another and had decided to travel around India together in search of more legal occupations.

Radhika was jittery. They still had 20 minutes to wait before the first train was due and the fear of being captured was overwhelming. How much longer before their absence was discovered? What if someone came after them? Would they be killed if they were caught? She knew her friends were thinking similar thoughts and tried to quell her own fears.

The girls began to talk about their dreams for the future. 'Radhika is sure to become a Bollywood star,' Reeta joked, 'She's studied the characters hard enough.'

'If Radhika is going to Bollywood, then you're going to Hollywood,' Riya teased Reeta, 'You've already achieved the impossible by getting us this far. Now, no stunt will be too big for you.'

Along with Radhika, Laxmi was the quiet member of the group but even she had her own take on Reeta's future career. 'Forget all that,' she said dryly, 'Reeta will go on to command the Indian army. She will come back in a tank and bulldoze every brothel in the land.'

Radhika's response was more profound. She told Reeta how much she admired her and shyly confided to this amazing girl that she was in awe of her courage and confidence, characteristics that had got the four girls and Rohan to this place. She owed her more than she could ever repay.

The girlish chatter helped to pass the time until they would depart on their journeys. An announcement over a loud speaker finally told Radhika that her train was ready to depart. With Rohan still asleep on her back, she hugged Laxmi, Reeta and Riya in turn.

As the tears streamed down her face, she told them: 'You have given my son the chance of a future. I can never repay you for that but I hope the Gods will do it for me. Good luck and stay together – you are [very] special.'

With those words ringing in their ears, the girls watched as Radhika summoned all the strength that she could muster to walk away from them. These three extraordinarily courageous girls had given her firstly the renewed hope she needed and then the courage and conviction to believe that this dream might work. That all four of them might finally escape. The girls' generosity simply couldn't be repaid, although Radhika vowed that she would try.

She hauled herself onto the train from the platform, clutching Rohan and their few belongings to her.

Her energy was waning. For some weeks Radhika had been suffering from a mild fever but the brothel owner had refused to call a doctor and she was now feeling quite dreadful. She struggled to keep focussed but she felt dizzy and very hot. Radhika tried to ignore the weakness in her body, putting it down to the immense stress of the moment.

Struggling through the carriage, past the families and friends who were settling themselves down for the long journey, Radhika managed to find two vacant seats next to a dusty, dirty window. She gently untied Rohan, holding him close as she put him down, careful not to disturb his sleep. He didn't stir and she thanked the gods again for keeping them safe thus far.

Radhika rested her head back against the seat. She took a deep breath. They had done it. It was over.

Rubbing her hands over her weary eyes, she shook her head, trying to clear her mind. She just had time to wave 'goodbye' to the girls, one last time.

Shakily, she got to her feet, steadying herself on the chair back in front of her as the carriage began to swim around her. She was just so tired. That was all. Glancing at her sleeping son, reassuring herself that Rohan was ok, she pushed past the other passengers, making her way down the carriage to the train window.

Leaning out of the window, she craned her head around to see if she could spot her friends. It was so crowded. There were so many people. She couldn't quite make them out.

Wait! Was that Reeta? Squinting, she peered into the murkiness of the station. The girls must all be so excited. Like Radhika and Rohan, they were all finally free.

Her feelings of elation quickly turned to terror. She couldn't believe her eyes. Unable to help herself, Radhika leaned as far forward as she could out of the train window. It couldn't be true? Fate couldn't be that cruel. She closed her eyes momentarily, hoping that it was all a bad dream, but when she opened them again the scene before her was still the same. There was no doubt in her mind what she was witnessing.

There on the platform, shoving and pushing people out the way, were the brothel Madame's henchmen. They had clearly seen her and were making their way through the crowd towards her. She quickly scanned the crowd, hoping beyond hope that the other girls had got away, then her eyes were drawn back to the three burly men who would reach her within seconds.

These thugs were notorious for the beatings they inflicted on the girls at the brothel with iron bars, barely hiding their joy when they drew blood. All the girls in the brothel had lived in fear of them. She knew that once they got her off the train it was all over.

Radhika quickly pulled her head back in from the window. She could still see the men from where she stood. She could also hear the soles of their shoes crashing down on the platform floor.

It had all been for nothing, then.

Her heart thundering against her chest, she tried to quell the utter despair she felt. Soon it would be over. She shut her eyes again, waiting for the moment when she would pulled from the train. Then something miraculous happened.

The train started to shudder, judder and sway. Radhika heard the screech of the engine – and held her breath as she felt the stirrings of new hope. Maybe, *just maybe*, the gods were watching her and Rohan after all. The train was beginning to move.

'Please! *Please* …,' she whispered desperately, aware that the men had almost reached her.

'Please, G–OOOO … G–OOO,' her whispers turned to shouts as the train suddenly lurched forward and began to gather proper speed just as Radhika's would-be captors leapt for the carriage door.

A final thrust of the engine and the train was properly on its way, steaming away from the platform, far too fast for anyone to board it. After a few seconds, Radhika leaned fully out of the train window to see the men still sprinting after her but the powerful engine was now too much for them.

She closed her eyes and then, taking a deep breath, screamed as loud as she could, careless of what anyone near her might think, venting all the pent-up anger and emotion of the recent years in captivity. The scream came from deep within her and seemed to last an age.

For a second she felt relief, then guilt overwhelmed her as she took the seat next to Rohan. She and Rohan were now free but what about their saviours Laxmi, Riya and Reeta? Had they managed to get away, too? Their trains hadn't arrived yet. She'd only just said goodbye to them before she'd boarded the train with Rohan. What if they were caught? What if they were being rounded up this second? What if they were dragged back to the brothel? Surely that couldn't happen? Surely the gods could not be that cruel?

As she sat in her seat on the train carrying her away from Mumbai, Radhika sank her head into her hands. She could only pray that her friends were also on the road to freedom. The alternative was simply too terrible to contemplate.

Redemption

RADHIKA'S heart was still beating fast as she sunk back into the seat next to her sleeping son and finally allowed herself to surrender to the moment.

Strangely, despite all the earlier terror, excitement and feelings of despair and hope, she now felt nothing. Trains had been trafficking her from one terrible tragedy to the next for almost three years and she was now approaching 21. The whirring of the wheels against the tracks had always sounded like a woeful symphony of sorrow, filling her with feelings of dread and uncertainty. Now Radhika felt numb to this sound and pretty much everything else as well. Only one emotion continued to overwhelm her completely – that of undying love for the small boy who lay curled up next to her.

She watched Rohan sleeping soundly and thought about the intensity of her love for him. It was only her unrelenting wish to be reunited with her precious son that had enabled Radhika to endure such extreme cruelty over the last few years.

For Rohan's sake, she had put up with being treated as less than human, just a piece of meat, an unwilling body for countless strangers to enjoy. And ultimately, he had been the catalyst for her agreement to be part of the girls' dangerous escape plan. She had been willing to take the risk that they might fail because the alternative – continuing to live in that hellhole and ultimately accepting it as their life – was something she couldn't contemplate. She would never accept the idea that Rohan might become that little boy she had seen playing in the sewage. She would rather kill them both.

The long journey home to Nepal was the final hurdle on the road to redemption for Radhika. But could she make it? Did she have the strength left to endure? She looked at her son and knew that she could bear anything for his sake.

From the first moment that Radhika had set eyes on him she felt a love that was so overwhelming it made her feel invincible. Back then, she could never have imagined the extent to which that love for her son would be tested. She had not only endured but, to a certain degree, she had conquered. She took a certain amount of pride from that.

While Radhika felt relieved to be on the way home, her physical pain and discomfort such that she knew a fairy-tale ending was still some way off. Her dizziness and nausea hadn't abated and her fever had, if anything, got worse. Also, watching Rohan, who was becoming increasingly disturbed as their journey progressed, she wondered if life would ever be 'normal' for them. Rohan would certainly need his mother's undivided love and attention for years to come if he was to achieve any degree of stability.

Between bouts of fitful sleep, her mind also kept wandering back to Reeta, Riya and Laxmi. Their loyalty and courage was beyond words and she could only pray, as she had done since the train had first left Mumbai, that they had escaped. If not, she hoped that they, too, would one day be free.

It was to be three long days and nights before the train eventually screeched to a halt in Gorakhpur in eastern Uttar

Pradesh. And before that, Radhika and Rohan still had much to endure. As she watched India's now familiar landscape flash past the train carriage window, she thought about her life to date. Was it any wonder she felt so ill? She had had to suffer so much both physically and mentally over the past years.

'I had not felt 100 percent healthy since the time my kidney was taken,' Radhika explains. 'The violence inflicted on me by my husband, Rajesh, served to weaken me further and the poverty that Rohan and I had endured meant that we would often go for whole days without any proper nutrition. Finally, the physical toll taken on my body in the brothels had left me close to collapse. I could feel a terrible fever welling up inside me but I had to keep fighting for Rohan's sake.'

Two hours into the journey to Gorakhpur on a cold December day, Rohan's eyes finally flickered open. Radhika says: 'He wasn't able to communicate with me in words because he had lost nearly all his ability to speak but I could tell by his eyes he was still very afraid.

'He had been on too many of these journeys before to trust that we were going anywhere other than another brothel. And for him this always meant being wrenched away from me and thrust into the hands of cruel strangers.

'I never got to see inside one of the compounds where Rohan was held captive but I had heard terrible stories of filthy living conditions and terrible beatings dished out to any child who dared to cry for its mother.

'The infected cigarette burn inside Rohan's mouth was a constant reminder of the terrible experiences he had endured. I knew his road to recovery was going to be a long one.'

A full day into the journey, a ticket inspector entered Radhika and Rohan's carriage and asked to see their travel documents. After giving them the obligatory stamp and exchanging pleasantries about the weather, he offered the desperate pair some food.

'I think he sensed we were very poor and maybe guessed that we were fleeing a terrible life. He had probably seen it all before on that particular train route. He seemed very kind and offered us bread and water.

'My faith in human nature had faltered long ago but I was in no position to refuse an offer of help … Rohan and I gladly accepted the food and ate it greedily.'

But barely five minutes after Radhika had filled her empty belly, she was violently sick. A distressed Rohan began to cry loudly and Radhika stood up quickly in an attempt to clear the mess. Blood began to gush out of her, soaking through her jeans, running onto the floor. She began to hear a loud ringing noise in her ears. It was to be the last thing she remembered. Darkness engulfed her as her last thoughts were of Rohan.

The familiar smell of disinfectant and the scraping of starched sheets against her skin made Radhika start to awakeness. She let out a loud scream.

For a moment she thought her life had come full circle and she was back in the Chennai hospital bed where she first discovered her kidney had been taken.

The memory of the ticket inspector suddenly flashed into consciousness. Had she been too trusting once again? Had the bread and water he had given her been laced with drugs? She struggled up. *Where was Rohan?*

Increasingly distressed, she tried to find some evidence of her son. She felt a reassuring hand on her shoulder and glancing up, she saw a nurse looking down at her, an expression of great kindness in her eyes. She placed a cold compress against Radhika's forehead, gently pressing the young woman back onto the bed.

'Please try to relax,' she told Radhika. 'You are very sick and we are taking care of you.'

Radhika recalls, 'I somehow knew instinctively that I was in good hands this time and I immediately believed what the nurse was telling me.

'I looked up to see Rohan being cuddled by another nurse at my bedside and told myself we were going to be ok. I finally sank back into my pillow and slept for what seemed like hours.'

A doctor later explained to Radhika that she had suffered a miscarriage, thus explaining the blood that had suddenly gushed from her body. To make matters worse, the fever was a symptom of typhoid. She was gravely ill and needed immediate treatment.

Radhika reveals: 'I wasn't shocked – just pleased to be alive. It wasn't the first miscarriage I had suffered since working in the brothels.

'The first time it happened I was shocked and distraught. I remember being in intense pain and bleeding profusely but I didn't know what was happening to my body until one of the other girls explained. I felt utterly bereft.

'Even though my pregnancy with Rohan had not been a happy one because of the way his father behaved, I felt so much love for the child inside me. I couldn't help thinking about that first child I lost and what he or she might have looked like or become. But there is little time to think when you are being trafficked from one customer and brothel to the next. As with many things, what you consider shocking in your previous life soon becomes worryingly normal in your new, sordid existence and before long, I began to view a miscarriage as a blessing. The children of India's brothels are caged in a living hell and how could I have wished that on yet another innocent life.'

She continues, 'Most of the Madames I worked for insisted on their prostitutes using protection but the condoms weren't always the best quality and sometimes they broke. I kept thinking how futile it would have been to fight so long for Rohan only to die on the train journey home. Somehow I had found the strength to pull through for him one last time. I couldn't thank the doctors and nurses enough for what they had done for us.

It felt like something in the planets was changing. For every evil person we had encountered over the past few years, a good soul was now being placed in our path.'

Radhika stayed in hospital for just one night before discharging herself and taking a rickshaw back to the station. She was so disorientated, she didn't even know where she was. She just boarded the next train to Gorakhpur, clutching Rohan and her bag of prescribed medication to her. Radhika still has no recollection of where that hospital was located, a place where the staff were so kind to her and Rohan. It was enough just to be alive.

After another day-and-a-half, mother and son finally reached Gorakhpur at 8 p.m. As the train finally stopped moving, Radhika closed her eyes. They had made it. They had finally made it. Now, anything was possible.

She tried not to think of her friends and where they might be. She had to remain positive. She dreamed that they, like her, had reached their destination. She imagined the three girls sitting in a cafe somewhere lovely, clean and light, excitedly planning their futures.

Radhika's thoughts quickly turned to the next stage of her journey home. From Gorakhpur, she would have to hitch a lift by bus or car to the Sunauli border. Only then could she and Rohan eventually cross over from India into Nepal and begin the final emotional pilgrimage home to Kathmandu and to her family.

But she was aware that something was wrong with her. Something serious. Her mind was still strong, but her body was failing her. She had only held on this long for Rohan but the truth was that she wasn't feeling at all well. With every passing minute she could feel her life force, her energy ebbing away.

Radhika had dreamed of this moment of freedom for so long. She desprately wanted to savour it – to celebrate with laughter or tears of joy – but physically she could feel her body shutting down. It was almost as if, after all this time, it was shouting, *'Enough!'*

Radhika felt disorientated in the darkness and symptoms of dizziness began to overwhelm her once more.

She recalls: 'I literally stumbled off the train with Rohan strapped to my back. We must have looked a terrible sight with our deathly pallor and dirty clothes.

'I gulped in the freezing [December] night air and immediately stumbled, feeling dizzy again. I saw a small kerbside ahead of us and managed to stagger over and sink down on it. Rohan was elated to be free from the confines of the train and immediately started running around.'

The little boy scampered about as Radhika rested her head on her knees. After a few seconds, with a great amount of effort, she raised it again, suddenly aware that she couldn't hear Rohan. Looking around her, she realized he was nowhere in sight. She glanced around her in growing panic. Where was he? *Where* was her son?

She tried to stand, but dizziness overwhelmed her. She couldn't breathe. She could feel her heart beating so loudly that the sound drowned out everything else. The world began to recede, disintegrating into a series of black dots. She forced herself to concentrate, mentally willing herself back to the real world.

A man appeared at the end on the platform. He strode towards her and gradually, she became aware that he carried her son in his arms.

As he came closer, she noted almost absently that Rohan wasn't struggling, so used was he to being handled by strangers. Stopping infront of her, with the boy held loosely in his arms, the man gently began to berate Radhika for her lack of parental control.

She says: 'He was concerned that [Rohan] would fall onto the train tracks and warned me to take better care of him. I explained that I was too weak to stand let alone run after my lively son.

'At this point he began looking at me more intently and something in his expression changed.'

The young man, Sushil, was in his late 20s, tall and handsome. He appeared to be an official of some sort. His smart uniform, leather boots and clean-cut appearance led Radhika to believe he might possibly have been a policeman. But she never got round to asking him. His profession made no difference to Radhika. She now felt so ill she actually believed that she was close to death. She was certainly in no mood to make small talk.

Sushil instinctively knew he had chanced upon someone desperately in need of help. But his reaction to what Radhika told him was extraordinary. She briefly outlined her experiences over the last three years, mindful that someone needed to know for Rohan's sake, in case something happened to her.

She says: 'He listened intently before pausing for a moment. Then he told me: "If you are prepared to trust someone just one last time, I will take you home."

'There was a soulfulness about him that made me think I could trust him, so I slowly nodded my head before bursting into tears.

'I had learned to handle cruelty but kindness had eluded me for so long – it made me feel very emotional. Anyway, however it turned out, I knew it was probably my last chance to make it home alive.'

Aware that she had made a lot of bad choices over the year and that she might be gambling with their lives again, Radhika drew in a breath. This time she felt it was right to trust this man, this stranger, with her and Rohan's lives. This time it was her choice.

Sushil wasted no time in gently scooping Rohan up into his strong arms and swinging him over his head onto his broad back. He took Radhika's small carrier bag in one hand and gently clasped her fingers with his other.

Radhika, feeling too ill to do otherwise, followed the tall man. He led the way to a parked jeep and carefully lifted

Radhika and Rohan into the back seats of the vehicle before he climbed into the driver's seat. He took them on a bumpy three-hour journey to the Sunauli border.

Radhika fell asleep, only waking when Sushil stopped the car at their destination.

Sushil carefully lifted mother and son out of the car and led them to a waiting bus. He shepherded Radhika onto the bus, still holding Rohan. He quickly found her two seats to stretch out on, and somewhat to her surprise also sat down with Rohan, the boy held protectively on his lap. He stayed with them, even when the bus started up and drove off.

Radhika had no idea why he was doing this. She and Rohan were strangers after all. It crossed her mind that he might be a trafficker, taking her back to the old gang, but she was too sick to develop that thought much further.

Halfway through the final, gruelling, 10-hour stretch home to Kathmandu, Radhika felt her strength returning and she began to feel more like her old self.

Sitting up, she began to talk to Sushil, sharing some of her more shocking experiences with the man. She found him surprisingly easy to talk to and he also encouraged her to speak, as if he were used to listening to other people's misery. She quickly found herself pouring her heart out to him. She told this stranger her entire life story, off-loading all the misery, the danger and then the hope to him.

'He seemed really saddened by what I was describing and kept on gravely shaking his head.

'In the beginning, it hadn't really occurred to me to ask him why he was helping us. I barely had the energy to speak. But now I could ask him the question I had been dying to ask, "Why do so much for strangers?" He simply replied that he felt he had no choice.

"What kind of a man would leave a mother and her child on the roadside like that? Not someone who could truly call himself a man," was his reply.

'He was very good with Rohan too. He played endless games of hide and seek using an old newspaper and Rohan was beginning to engage with him and even make some sounds. It was an amazing sight to see him smile again.'

This level of kindness was almost beyond belief to Radhika. This stranger was more like the men she had grown up with, men like her father. The men who she had almost forgotten existed, such had been her experiences in the last few years.

She closed her eyes and thanked the gods for watching over her and Rohan. They were almost home.

At around 11 a.m., Radhika, Rohan and Sushil finally reached Kathmandu's central bus station.

Radhika couldn't believe the journey was almost over. Tears welled up in her eyes as she slowly disembarked from the rickety bus and took in the familiar smells and sounds of her homeland.

It was almost three years since she had last stood on Nepalese soil and she doubted her son had any memories of their native country.

She found herself drinking in every smell, every colour, every sign of humanity on the bustling, dusty streets – elated to feel a sense of belonging once more.

Finally, when she had the strength to take Rohan from Sushil's arms, Radhika gathered her tiny son to her.

She looked gratefully at the man who had helped her complete this journey before whispering in Rohan's ear. 'We're home, darling. We're finally *HOME*.'

Coming home

WITH Sushil by her side and Rohan in her arms, Radhika felt like an exiled princess returning to her homeland – even after everything she had been through.

For years she had been regarded as little more than human flesh, traded and trafficked around India in exchange for a few thousand rupees. Now, back safely in Nepal she finally felt human again.

Radhika imagined for a moment what it would feel like to call Sushil her husband and felt her cheeks burning as they turned red. This handsome stranger had saved her life on a kerbside in India and now he was fulfilling his promise to take her home. Surely there was something more to this than mere chance? Was Sushil her destiny? It was a whimsical idea for a girl who had been through as much as she had done and for a brief moment she allowed herself to indulge in what might have been. But in truth, romance was the last thing on Radhika's mind. She was elated to be back in the land of her birth although physically she felt wrecked.

Sushil sensed Radhika's fatigue and immediately summoned a taxi. Nepal's unique landscape had been a stranger to Radhika for so long. Now the sight of the majestic Himalaya mountains caused her to burst into tears. How could such a beautiful and spiritual country have produced the kind of men and women who had almost destroyed her? It was a question she felt sure she would never be able to answer.

As the dilapidated Lada taxi weaved its way out of the bustling city towards Radhika's home village of Kavresthali, it passed through Balaju, alongside the Bishnumati River. It was there, six years ago, that Radhika had unwittingly been drawn into the evil world of human trafficking.

As she passed the young girls selling vegetables, just as she had done, Radhika felt a shiver go down her spine as she recalled that time. She had been *so* innocent, happily accepting Sanjay Lama's offers of friendship and then of lucrative work at face value. How could she have possibly known what would happen to her? She had been extremely naive.

It was little wonder that she had become so distrustful of the male sex given her encounters with the Pariyars, her husband and the men she had encountered at the brothels, although Jigmi was the exception. Then, in her hour of need, a good Samaritan in the form of Sushil had turned up to help her. Radhika felt sure that the gods were trying to send her a message – perhaps they were attempting to restore her faith in the world.

Radhika recalls: 'The journey home had been long but I felt elated to be back in my own country again. I kept looking across at Rohan. He was just a year old when we were trafficked to India for the first time and he had no recollection of his birth country.

'He still said nothing but I could see that his eyes were soaking up the brightly coloured kurtas and breathtaking landscape through the window of the taxi.

'It seemed unbelievable that I had once taken Nepal for granted. The journey from Mumbai had taken over five days but every second was worth the discomfort that Rohan and I had endured.

'Every mile had taken us further from India's brothel landscape and closer to this paradise.'

Radhika now viewed her homeland through the eyes of both a native and a tourist, drinking in its awesome beauty with new eyes. Crowned by 8 of the world's 10 highest mountains, its rugged terrain combines lush tropics and artic tundra. From the terraced valleys to the forested hills, frozen peaks and elevated mountain deserts – Radhika wanted to savour every aspect of the land she had been so cruelly snatched from.

Out of the corner of her eye she caught a glimpse of a beautiful blue pheasant and watched as it foraged for food before spreading its wings and flying off into the distance. She could not recall seeing a bird like this in Kathmandu before. Perhaps it was a sign that she was finally free.

'Sushil also said very little. He just [watched] our faces and smiled. He seemed delighted to be part of our homecoming and told me [that] I should not feel ashamed of anything that had happened to me no matter what my family or the villagers might say.

'I had no idea what sort of reception we were going to get but I sensed that Sushil was preparing me for the worst.

'It didn't really matter. I still felt gravely ill and was only focussed on making it home alive. Even if my health [failed] … at least Rohan would be with people who [would] love and cherish him.'

On the outskirts of the city, an increasingly rough terrain was causing the impatient, middle-aged taxi driver to grumble. After letting out a stream of expletives, some of which Radhika hadn't heard in Nepali before, but all directed at the state of his suspension, the man swerved the vehicle to a stop at the side of the unsurfaced road. They waited to see what would happen next. After a few moments, he swore again before demanding payment from them and ordering them out of the car.

Radhika, Rohan and Sushil had little choice other than to obey. They slowly disembarked and found themselves beside the majestic and breathtaking entrance to Swayambhunath.

The ancient religious site sits majestically on top of a hill to the west of Nepal's capital, in Kathmandu Valley. The Rhesus Macaque that occupy the complex's shady crevices also give it the name Monkey Temple. It is arguably the most sacred of all Buddhist pilgrimage sites but is also revered by Hindus and consists of stupa and a variety of intricately painted shrines and temples.

Some of the world's more discerning tourists mingle with the local Hindu and Buddhist devotees who flock each day to the site to drink in its magical aura. A heady smell of incense wafts across the base of the temple and sets the scene for the majestic climb to the top where pilgrims can finally absorb the essence of one of the world's most fascinating religions.

Here, amid ancient religious relics, sit serene-faced monks dressed in bright red and orange robes. Some sleep outside the temples, among the sea of souvenir stalls selling glossy peacock feathers and replica stupas. Despite this, silence prevails, except for the interruption of the distant but entrancing whir of the prayer wheels turned thousands of times daily. The beautifully embossed, metal cylinders are mounted on a rod handle and contain a tightly wound scroll printed with a mantra. According to Tibetan Buddhist belief, spinning a prayer wheel is just as effective as reciting the sacred texts aloud.

Coming Home

Radhika watched spellbound as devout Buddhist and Hindu pilgrims paid homage to the temple. Serene-faced men and women began the steep ascent of 365 steps past the gilded *vajra* (the short, metal weapon symbolizing spiritual power) and the two lions guarding the entrance.

Radhika recalled the history of the temple from school. Now, she delighted in relaying it to Sushil.

'Apparently the entire Kathmandu Valley was once filled with a vast lake and out of it grew a beautiful lotus. The valley came to be known as Swayambhu (self-created). I felt proud telling Sushil about my heritage. At least he would see there was more to me than a naive farmer's daughter who had allowed herself to be sold into the brothels of India.

'And it seemed more than a mere coincidence that the driver had dropped us near the temple. Here, right in front of me was another reminder that I could renew my faith in the world,' Radhika comments.

Now on foot, a weak Radhika had to steel herself to walk the final 5km (3.1 miles) to freedom. Sushil linked his arm in hers, giving her his strength, and placed Rohan on his back as they trekked slowly along the narrow, twisting roads to Radhika's home village.

The terrain was uneven and difficult to negotiate in her exhausted state but even so she could tell that the landscape was changing, becoming more familiar. The lush, green reaches of the Himalaya and vast areas of brown mud-topped farmland were the plains of her childhood. Familiar flowers in every colour of the rainbow burst out of the ground making the vista indescribably beautiful. The sound of the cows and goats baying at each other was the only noise that punctuated the silence. This was what Radhika recalled on the most hellish of nights in the brothels. When she could manage to transport herself back to this stunning landscape, it was all slightly more bearable.

Then suddenly there it was, her family home. She had to blink rapidly, so frightened was she that it was all a dream and she would wake up to find herself and Rohan back in the Mumbai brothel.

'Sushil squeezed my arm and told me to carry on walking as best as I could manage.'

The young man took care of her, giving her the strength to face her family, even though she wasn't sure what lay ahead or how she would be received.

Taking a deep breath, she led the way forward to where her parents stood, watching the little group make their way slowly towards them.

Maiya and Ramprasad were outside their small mud house tending the spinach patch when they heard voices signifying visitors. They watched as the young girl, man and boy climbed the hill towards them. They couldn't quite make out who any of them were, the sun was behind them, but there was something familiar about the way the girl moved, something that made Maiya's chest tighten.

As Radhika drew closer to her parents, she could see their faces more clearly. They had changed very little, Radhika thought. Perhaps they had a few more lines, here and there, from their daily toil in the sun, but essentially her parents looked the same as when she had left home, aged just 14 years old. The years had been kind to them. They wore the same warm smiles with which they always greeted people. She was aware of the moment that her mother recognized her.

'My mother looked at me as if she had seen a ghost. We just stood there for a few seconds [all] frozen before she ran towards [us], her arms outstretched.

'I was still very sick and we were filthy. I must have looked a shocking sight but I could feel instantly that the love between us was still there. Of course, lots of questions [were] being fired at me but I was too ashamed to tell my parents the truth, so I lied to them and said I had been working in a carpet factory in India.

'I wanted to reveal our true ordeal but [I] didn't have the courage and I knew they wouldn't understand anyway. They assumed Sushil was my boyfriend and that we had been having an affair, but I set them straight and explained that he had simply found me near to death from typhoid at a train station and offered to accompany me home. It sounded unbelievable as I said it but, of course, it was true.'

Radhika's elated parents started to usher their beloved daughter into the house – but another family member blocked her path. Radhika's beloved grandmother, Hari Prem, could barely look the young woman in the eye.

Radhika explains: 'She was the undisputable head of the village community. She told me she was willing to forgive my long absence from home without contact, but could not forgive the fact that I had married someone of a lower caste.

'Her word was final. Rohan and I would not be allowed entry into the house and would have to sleep on a cement ledge outside, with only a single wool blanket for warmth. She felt that anything else would bring bad luck upon the family. If only she knew how much bad luck had come my way already.'

After everything Radhika and Rohan had been through, an outsider might expect her family to have rallied around her. Sushil certainly was shocked by her reception but traditional Nepalese society frowns on intercaste marriage, even if it's forced, and Radhika had to face the reactions of people who truly believed that through such a marriage she had not only brought disgrace to her family but had tainted them as well.

The caste system is still deeply entrenched in Nepal and India that it may take one or two more generations before women like Radhika are free from the stigma of marrying outside their particular caste. Even talking about intercaste and inter-religion marriages in Nepal is taboo for many people and in villages, daughters are at best disowned or at worst murdered or brutally tortured, along with other family members, for entering into an intercaste marriage.

In 2009, the Nepalese government announced that they would give 100,000 NPR (about £900) to couples from different castes entering marriage. The gesture was aimed at helping end discrimination against the country's Dalits (the so-called 'Untouchable' caste), who still face discrimination. Radhika's experience proves the problem is far less simple to resolve. 'Who wants to be rich if they are cut off from their family? The money will go [and] you are left with nothing.'

It may seem strange but Radhika understands Hari Prem's reaction to her marriage. 'I was upset but not shocked by my grandmother's reaction. Later, my parents told me that the local villagers had found out about my marriage and that they would not even share the same water supply if I went inside the house. Some even said I should be killed.

'I didn't really care what they said about me ... but I was concerned for Rohan. He had been treated so badly by so many strangers – how would he feel knowing his own flesh and blood was shunning him, too?

Hari Prem explains: 'We need each other for everything up here in these villages. I couldn't accept Radhika because I was afraid that the entire village would go against us. I have always felt a great love for Radhika and now for Rohan too but I am afraid of going against tradition. Where would we go if were were forced to leave our village?'

Sushil tried to intervene but Radhika told him to stay out of it. Amazingly, Hari Prem welcomed Sushil inside the family home and allowed him to sleep off his fatigue for two nights. She invited him to stay longer, but he insisted that it was time for him to return to his responsibilities in India.

Sushil departed one morning after taking a drink of warm milk from the Phuyal family cow. He went first to Rohan and swept him off the ground before giving him a big hug, whispering, 'Good luck little one. Take care of your mother.'

Then he turned to Radhika, squeezing her hands tightly in his. As she instinctively thanked him for all he had done for her and Rohan, Sushil hushed her, saying, 'I've already told you from the start, I need no thanks. What I did, I did for you because I wanted to and it has been a privilege to help you. You are a true survivor and I wish you all the luck and happiness in the world. But promise me … never, ever trust a stranger again. From now on, try to be the master of your own destiny.'

With that, he turned his back and began striding down the hill path that he had helped Radhika up only a few days earlier. He stopped halfway down, turning back briefly to wave at the boy and his mother. Then he was gone from sight, as gracefully as he had come. Sushil, their saviour.

When Sushil left, Radhika was, in fact, too ill to really feel anything other than relief that she was finally home with Rohan. She was aware that Sushil had done something that was quite extraordinary. He was the reason that she was here in the heart of her family. When he left she certainly didn't feel abandoned by him, just extremely sad that she might never see him again. He had done her a great service that she simply couldn't repay.

Radhika had dreamed of returning home for years. For a long time it had been just that, a dream, but Sushil had helped make it possible. Like Jigmi, Reeta, Laxmi and Riya, through his extreme kindness, Radhika and Rohan had a chance of a new life.

Back home, she had a million questions to ask her family and a million things to tell them. She wanted to hug them, drink in their presence, study their features and see how they had changed, but she was finding it difficult to focus on anything. Radhika's health was deteriorating once again. She had not been able to shake off the symptoms of typhoid – and her miscarriage was also causing her to bleed profusely again. Moreover, sleeping outdoors was exacerbating her symptoms and her temperature was fluctuating greatly.

Luckily, another saviour emerged just in time. Word of Radhika's return had reached her sister, Parvati, in Kathmandu. She wasted no time in getting a taxi to Kavresthali.

When she arrived, Parvati was deeply shocked by what she saw. As she recalls the moment she set eyes on her sister after all that time, her eyes fill with tears:

'I had always believed that Radhika's husband had returned to her after Rohan's birth and had taken his wife and child to another part of Nepal for a better life.

'Well, perhaps that's what I *wanted* to believe. The alternatives were too painful to contemplate. I just hoped that Radhika was happy and felt sure that she would get in touch when she felt ready. I was certainly not prepared for the sight that greeted me.

'Radhika [seemed] close to death and was bleeding profusely. Her bleeding was so bad; she looked like she had been in a traffic accident. And Rohan [was] severely traumatized. 'He wasn't even able to speak because of an inexplicable injury on his tongue and he appeared to understand only Hindi and no Nepali. He was also experiencing severe memory loss.

'Radhika was still insisting she had been working in a carpet factory but I sensed there was more to her trauma so I persuaded her to come back to Kathmandu with me to convalesce in my home. I knew my husband wouldn't be happy but how could our own flesh and blood be forced to sleep outside in the cold? I was afraid Radhika might die.'

Back at Parvati's family home, Radhika finally confessed her horrific experiences to her elder sister. For months, she had agonized about how she could tell her family the true sordid story of what had happened to her since leaving Nepal that first time.

She wondered if it was better to spare them the pain of knowing what had really happened to her and Rohan, if it was better just to keep silent and pretend that she had been pursuing legitimate work opportunities. In the end, she couldn't bear the burden of keeping it to herself any longer. She knew there was an element of risk involved in divulging the brutal facts to Parvati. Her sister could blame Radhika for being naive and stupid, for bringing shame on the Phuyal name, but in the end Radhika knew that the truth had to come out and Parvati had, in recent years at least, proved herself a friend as well as a good sister.

Radhika recalls, 'One night when her husband was out working at his bag factory, I broke down and told her everything. She told me that I should not be afraid because she would support me and stand by me ... Ever since then, she has been true to her word.'

They decided to go to the police together. Surely they could do something to prevent this from happening to other girls? Radhika felt strongly that she had to speak about her experiences, no matter how difficult it was. She felt a duty to Laxmi, Reeta and Riya. She felt a duty to herself and to Rohan to do so.

But when Parvati and Radhika eventually made it to the police station in Kathmandu, they were horrified by their reception. After haltingly telling her story, gently coaxed on by Parvati, who sat clutching her hand, Radhika watched the tired-looking officers slouched across the desk from them. Their stance wasn't encouraging – if anything they seemed bored. They had glanced at one another when Radhika began recounting her excruciating story.

One of them smirked before commenting on her ordeal: 'Really? That must have been terrible for you and the tens of other women who come in here and say the same thing.

'What do you expect [to happen to you] if you disappear with a stranger in the dead of night? Foolish woman!'

Radhika and Parvati stared back at the man in shock. He made it sound as if it was her fault that she had been trafficked? As if what she had told him was really unimportant and she was wasting his time. Whatever Radhika had expected it wasn't that response.

The two women left the station completely disheartened. If the police weren't willing to do anything to stop this horrific practice from happening, how would it ever end? Then, Parvati had the idea of going to Krishna 'Purne' Pariyar's house.

Radhika knew roughly where he lived and after asking around found out exactly where his house was. She wasn't sure what to do when she and Parvati reached there, standing outside the gate, looking at the building that Pariyar had most probably bought with the proceeds from his trafficking. In the end, Parvati spurred her on, her sister's presence giving Radhika the strength to knock on the door.

When it opened a woman stood there, looking out at them suspiciously. She informed them that her husband was out. She struck Radhika as a good religious woman, slightly pious and it was this that Parvati ended up playing on. She told the woman that if she knew about her husband's crimes and didn't come forward then she would have terrible karma. In her next lives, Parvati added, she would be punished if she failed to do the right thing.

After some time, the woman gave in. Parvati and Radhika accompanied her back to the police station and encouraged her to report her husband's trafficking crimes.

'But still no one helped us,' Radhika comments bitterly.

However, this time as they were leaving the station for the second and last time, the gods again, it seemed to Radhika, intervened to help her and Rohan.

'[A] man came in to report a traffic accident,' Radhika recalls. 'He saw how distressed we were and asked if he could help us. We told him how I had fallen prey to human traffickers and he advised us to go immediately to a refuge called "Maiti Nepal". He gave us the address and wished us good luck.

'By now I had lost everything – my friends, my family and my innocence, but I still had a child to take care of. I had no choice but to head into the unknown one last time.

'We left the police station, hailed a taxi and handed the driver the address for Maiti Nepal.

'"No need," he responded politely, waving the piece of paper away. He knew where the refuge was. "It is becoming very well known," [he added].'

Bundled into the back of the taxi with Rohan and Parvati, Radhika mentally braced herself for further disappointment and heartache. What if they were again refused help? Could she bear it? This was, after all, their last chance.

An unexpected sanctuary

THE large iron gates of Maiti Nepal swung open and a woman of tiny stature, but great presence, greeted Radhika warmly. With outstretched arms, she beckoned Radhika and Rohan forward, grasping them both firmly but gently in a warm hug.

'Welcome. My name is Anuradha Koirala and Maiti Nepal will be your home for as long as you wish.'

The woman's manner was immediately reassuring. After her reception at the police station, Radhika had felt nervous about going to the refuge in central Kathmandu. Even with her sister beside her to hold her hand, she was deeply afraid. She had lost a great deal of trust in human nature and this was a huge leap of faith given everything she had been through. But what choice did she have but to accept charity if necessary? She couldn't live with her family and she was well aware that Rohan needed stability and sanctuary.

Unbeknown to Radhika, Parvati had already made a brief call to the refuge, informing staff of her sister's plight. Maiti Nepal's healing process immediately swung into action. For the first time in years, Radhika felt tempted to relax. There was something about this woman, even though she had never set on eyes on her before, that inspired trust.

And she needed to entrust herself and Rohan into someone else's care. After all the heartache and rejection, her experiences at the hands of the police, she needed someone to be kind to them.

And now, thanks to a chance encounter, Lady Luck, the gods, whatever one might choose to call it, had led Radhika and Rohan to true sanctuary. They had truly been transported somewhere safe, into the hands of one of the leading human rights activists in South Asia.

Sensing Radhika's disquiet, Anuradha placed a reassuring arm around the young girl's shoulders and asked her to sign the entry book.

Scratching *Radhika Phuyal* and the date *24 April 2008* on the page, she felt finally as if she could let go of the bitterness, the heartache, the unhappiness. Her four-year-old son's hand clasped tightly in her own, she looked into the warm brown eyes of the woman hugging her.

Radhika closed her eyes, finally able to acknowledge that she and Rohan had found a home.

The diminuitive lady who had met them so welcomingly at the gates to the refuge's compound was Anuradha Koirala, the founder and executive director of Maiti Nepal.

This former English teacher started Maiti (which means 'mother's home' in Nepali) in 1993. Anuradha's own history in an abusive relationship led her to set up this groundbreaking venture. For most of her young adulthood, she taught primary school English in Nepal, but when her own marriage became violent, her life's purpose and responsibility completely changed. After that relationship ended, Anuradha used a portion of her £68 per month salary to start a small retail shop employing and supporting displaced victims of sex trafficking and domestic violence. At the same time she was raising her son, Manish, now 29, single-handedly.

By the early 1990s, an increasing demand for help and persistent cases of violence against women compelled Anuradha to do more. Maiti Nepal was her brainchild for giving voice, legal representation and rehabilitation to victims of sex trafficking. The charity now has facilities throughout Nepal and India, but most of the rehabilitation work takes place at its main site in Kathmandu.

Anuradha says: 'When a girl first comes to Maiti Nepal ... we just let her [be] for as long as she needs. We let her play, dance, walk, talk to a friend. Like Radhika, many girls are afraid at first, but eventually they will talk to us.'

The group also takes in rape and domestic violence survivors, as well as abandoned children.

For years, Anuradha was shunned by Nepalese society who frowned on her activities, believing she was sullying her reputation by mixing with 'unclean' people. But she remained undeterred. The crusading 59-year-old has transformed countless lives with the project. 'Everybody comes to Maiti Nepal.'

Today, she is a widely recognized activist, who has dedicated her life to combatting the sexual exploitation of women and children. Accommodating the many people who need help requires a large staff of teachers, counsellors and medical personnel – and dozens of bunk beds. Many of the staff are sex-trafficking survivors now committed to helping rehabilitate other girls. The work is funded by grants and donations from around the world. Post-rescue recovery is comprehensive. Maiti Nepal provides medical treatment, psychological and legal counselling, formal court filings and criminal prosecution, all for free.

It houses 83 women and 252 children, including orphans of the Maoist war (the conflict between government forces and Maoist rebels in Nepal, which lasted from 1996 until 2006). Among the children, 24 are HIV positive, infected from their mothers, who were trafficked into brothels.

When Radhika arrived at the refuge, she like the many girls and children before her, immediately sensed that she was in the presence of someone great, someone who could help turn her life around.

She says: 'Anuradha was caring but firm and she seemed to know exactly what to do. I thought we might head straight to our room but she knew what was most important.

'She first took us to the legal section [of Maiti Nepal] and asked me to give a statement about my experiences.

'I was very nervous and scared but somehow I instinctively trusted her to do the right thing. I tried to recall the events of the past seven years as best as I could and it actually felt like a release to remember.'

Anuradha had heard many trafficking stories over the years but Radhika's struck her as particularly poignant.

'I feared initially that Radhika was a lost cause. She was broken and Rohan was absolutely lost. He wouldn't speak to anybody and was constantly hiding. I knew there was a lot of work ahead of us,' she remembers.

Radhika believes that her healing process started from the moment she was shown to her room at Maiti Nepal.

'After giving my statement, I said an emotional goodbye and thanks to my sister Parvati, and Rohan and I were led through the main grounds of Maiti Nepal. It is set around a beautiful grass courtyard with trees and flowers everywhere. I immediately felt at home and could even sense that Rohan was beginning to relax. We were sharing a lovely, airy room with five other women and children who had been trafficked in a similar way. Immediately, it made us feel "normal" and not like the "outcasts" we had become in my home village.

'We slept soundly that night. It felt wonderful to have Rohan by my side at last snuggling into my body. I drifted off to sleep thinking: "I kept my promise to my son. We are together again."

'I felt good about myself for the first time in years.'

Maiti Nepal runs on a strict timetable and Radhika and Rohan were woken for breakfast the next morning at 5 a.m. They attended a yoga class between 5.30 a.m. and 6 a.m. and were asked to participate in the daily cleaning duties between 6 a.m. and 7 a.m.

After the 7.30 a.m. breakfast meal of hot milk and bread, Anuradha appeared and asked Radhika to brace herself for a difficult day. She asked her to entrust Rohan to some of Maiti's trained careworkers while she and Radhika set to work. They climbed into one of the organization's 4x4 vehicles and headed into the city. This 'work' could be dangerous. They were going to hunt for Radhika's traffickers.

Radhika and Anuradha sat in the back of the Land Cruiser, while a driver began weaving his way through Kathmandu's congested, dusty roads in search of the traffickers' hideouts.

Recalling that drive, Radhika says, 'It was terrifying to be confronted with these memories again but Anuradha explained to me that she needed to know their addresses in order to tell police to arrest them.

'I pointed the addresses out one by one with shaking hands. None of them were at home that morning but Anuradha returned with her driver in the afternoon and found 'Purne' Pariyar. He had clearly conspired with my husband to kidnap me and sell me onto the brothels of India. Later, he was arrested on human trafficking charges.'

Radhika watched incredulously as this tiny woman, whom she had only met the day before, took up her fight. 'I couldn't believe that someone as important as Anuradha was getting involved in my case so personally. It made me feel very safe and protected.'

Back at Maiti Nepal, Anuradha's legal team began preparing a case against Pariyar while piecing together the complex jigsaw puzzle of Radhika's trafficking experiences. Meanwhile, Radhika and Rohan were allowed to get on with the business of healing. Mother and son sought solace in the love and care of Maiti's dedicated social workers, who help the survivors of human trafficking to come to terms with their experiences through counselling. And Rohan began attending the adjacent St Teresa's Academy school for the first time, fulfilling Radhika's dream for him to be educated.

While rehabilitation is central to Maiti Nepal's work, Anuradha is also focused on the wider problem of human trafficking. She informed Radhika that she had ordered police to bring Pariyar to Maiti Nepal for identification purposes.

After her recent experiences with the police, when they had appeared so dismissive, Radhika wondered how Anuradha could have such sway. How important she must be to get them to listen to her, she mused. This reinforced

Radhika's conviction that by coming to Maiti Nepal, her and Rohan's lives would change forever. What had seemed all but impossible when she and Rohan had left the police station with Parvati in tow, was now *more* than possible. Anuradha had restored her sense of hope.

Anuradha informed Radhika that if 'Purne' Pariyar had trafficked Radhika and Rohan, the chances were that he had done the same to many other women and children before and since then. The operation had been too seamless to think otherwise. And the network of interlinked brothels from which Radhika was transported across India, seemed to confirm that the trafficking operation was a large-scale one. Asking Maiti Nepal's residents to identify Pariyar might just give Anuradha the confirmation she needed.

Radhika recalls: 'Soon after Anuradha had sought him out, Pariyar was brought to Maiti Nepal for identification purposes. Anuradha asked me to stand on the grass in the courtyard along with 40 other girls and wait for him to be brought out in front of us.

'I immediately froze as I saw the familiar, arrogant face and wiry frame being marched towards me. He was sweating profusely and his floppy black hair stuck awkwardly to his face. Even his expensive-looking shirt and trousers were covered in sweat patches.

'He was clearly terrified to be confronted by his victims.

'For a moment, I felt so alone gazing at the man who had almost succeeded in destroying my son and I. [We were] terrified to see him again. I went completely numb and began to hear the familiar ringing sound in my ears, which told me I was about to faint.

'But then a louder sound began to drown out the ringing. It was the voices of some of the other girls around me shouting angrily at Pariyar. "You bastard," they yelled in unison, "Go to hell, you bastard".

'It suddenly dawned on me that they, too, had identified him as their trafficker. This wasn't just about me. He was clearly a well-known operator in this evil business.

'Then the crowd of girls around me began to surge forward. They couldn't contain their anger any longer and ran at him, launching severe blows on his body and head. Like me, many of them had been broken by the trafficking experiences they had been forced to endure – now they were intent on breaking the culprit.

'I wanted to vent my anger on him too but for some reason I couldn't. I just stood there watching the events around me as if they were in slow motion.

'My legs were still frozen but suddenly my mouth opened and I let out a piercing scream.'

As the high pitched sound reverberated round Maiti Nepal's courtyard, Radhika finally recognized that she was on the road to her own recovery. Her scream was the sound of freedom.

Epilogue

RADHIKA and Rohan remain at Maiti Nepal, where they continue to make huge strides forward, in the journey towards rehabilitation and some semblance of a normal life. This is where I first met them, when I found myself in Kathmandu in July 2009, sent by *The Sun* to cover the Gurkha Justice Campaign. Along with 15 other journalists and photographers, I accompanied the actress and campaigner Joanna Lumley from the capital to Jhapa, Pokhara, Dharan and back again, witnessing first-hand the overwhelming gratitude shown to Joanna following her much publicized UK campaign for Gurkha rights. On the last day of our week-long trip Joanna announced her intention to visit a Kathmandu shelter for trafficked women called Maiti Nepal and I asked if I could join her.

Joanna went on ahead of me and I arrived just as a group of trafficking survivors were about to perform a poignant Nepalese dance depicting the pain of their experiences. I shuffled quickly to the back of the audience, where Maiti Nepal's founder Anuradha Koirala soon sought me out. *Sun* journalists had previously visited the refuge while on a royal tour with Prince Charles and had subsequently embarked on a campaign that ended up funding part of an accommodation block for the refuge.

After speaking with Anuradha, I readily agreed to help as much as I could. I asked to meet a girl who best summed up the experience of human trafficking, promising that I would do my best to get her story published to raise awareness and more money for the shelter. Anuradha rushed off and moments later Radhika appeared with her son, Rohan, in tow. While her beauty and gentle demeanour were striking, her obvious love for her son was quite mesmerizing. We ended up sitting cross-legged on a lawn outside the refuge compound where she proceeded to tell me one of the most astonishing stories that I have heard in my career as a journalist. I sat spellbound for over two hours – in parts shocked, in parts almost paralyzed with disbelief but always intensely aware of the strong bond between Radhika and her son. Afterwards, I thanked Radhika for sharing her life story with me and returned to my hotel room, where I cried. It is rare to be so moved by a story after so many years in journalism but I knew that it was special and most importantly that it had to reach a greater audience.

Over the months since that first meeting, I have got to know Radhika and Rohan much better and have come to recognize the vital work that Maiti Nepal is doing in helping Radhika, Rohan and countless others reach some kind of resolution about their experiences, some so horrific that they still cannot be spoken about. By supplying peaceful and nurturing surroundings and training the girls and women who end up there to carry on with their schooling or to train in new areas – Radhika, for example, makes beautiful, beaded jewellery for export to America and also participates in daily Nepalese dance classes – Anuradha and her dedicated team help them regain their sense of self-worth and self-respect. The refuge places great emphasis on helping women to become economically self-sufficient, offering professional and vocational training in hairdressing, beauty therapy, floriculture, advanced sewing and bakery, among other things. It actively seeks placements for them and provides them with seed money to start up business enterprises, where appropriate.

Similarly, the children at the refuge benefit from the opportunities offered there. Rohan also attends Maiti Nepal's St Teresa's Academy. First established in 1998 by the refuge, it sits within the Maiti Nepal compound in Kathmandu and provides a formal, comprehensive education to those aged between five and 12. More than 150 children currently attend. Rohan has taken great strides forward and now speaks clearly and confidently. However, he does remain badly scarred by his trafficking experiences and Anuradha believes that he is in desperate need of help from a child psychologist, a service that she would like to be able to offer to all of the child survivors of trafficking.

But Anuradha's work does not stop with rehabilitation of the survivors of human trafficking. She also wages an active war against the problem on several other fronts. She orchestrates comprehensive awareness campaigns in remote villages – warning vulnerable, uneducated girls of the dangers of being tricked into prostitution. She also helps to bring the traffickers themselves to prosecution in court. Hence, Maiti Nepal has a well established on-site legal department staffed by dedicated lawyers, a team from which Radhika and Rohan have also benefitted. Its lawyers discovered that Radhika's husband, Rajesh Pariyar, was already in Kathmandu's Central Prison on alleged trafficking charges by the time Radhika returned from India to Nepal in 2007. They also helped build a case against Rajan Pariyar and Krishna 'Purne' Pariyar who were both imprisoned in Nepal after Radhika courageously gave evidence against them in a court on 2 November 2009.

On 1 June 2010, Radhika and Rohan saw both men convicted on human trafficking charges at the Kathmandu District Court, Rajan sentenced to 18 years and Purne to four years. As this book goes to press, Rajesh Kumar still awaits trial.

RADHIKA'S STORY

As for Radhika, I returned with her to Kavresthali to visit her family. Although Hari Prem's attitude towards her granddaughter's intercaste marriage holds firm, Radhika's parents state that situation will change once their respected matriarch passes away. Radhika's sister, Parvati, continues to be a constant source of love and strength. She visits Radhika and Rohan regularly at the refuge, the home to which she helped bring them.

While *Radhika's Story* is not easy to read, it was even harder to live. Radhika and Rohan did so and have survived – almost against the odds. While her experiences plunged this courageous young woman into a world of darkness, she encountered truly exceptional people who were willing to risk their lives for her and Rohan – proving that good can triumph over evil, even an evil as overwhelming as human trafficking.

Radhika constantly thinks about those who were instrumental in helping save her and Rohan. She wonders what happened to Jigmi and prays he is still alive. Reeta, Riya and Laxmi remain the most inspirational characters she will ever meet but Radhika is still concerned about whether they escaped the brothel henchmen who nearly thwarted her own dash for freedom. She will only sleep easy once she knows that they are safe and alive. And she would love to be reunited with Sushil, not just to thank him properly, but also to allow him to see that she and Rohan are well and thriving.

Most inspirational of all in this story is Radhika herself and the love she has for Rohan. That love ultimately helped her survive the awful situations she was placed in and also, through the actions and help of the very fine people who aided her, enabled her finally to bear witness to the conviction of some of the traffickers who tried – and failed – to bring Radhika, Rohan, and so many others, before and after them, down.

Disclaimer

The description of events and interactions in this book are the product of the author's interpretation and dramatization of information provided to her via public records, media reports and interviews. The author has drawn her own conclusions with regard to such information and whilst these might be regarded by the reader as representing, in all instances, the factual recording of events, they are not, and should not be interpreted as such. Moreover, during many of the events depicted in the book, Radhika was understandably disoriented, exhausted and confused. That fact, coupled with her lack of previous travel much beyond the village in which she lived, results in some uncertainty with respect to precise geographical locations and specific timeframes. It has no bearing on the reality of the trauma that she endured.

Thank you.

Further Information

Please see the following websites to find out more about human trafficking in the modern world.

Maiti Nepal
www.maitinepal.org

Friends of Maiti Nepal
www.friendsofmaitinepal.org

Ecpat – End Child Prostitution, Child Pornography and Trafficking of Children for Sexual Purposes International
www.ecpat.net

The Rescue Foundation – A Mumbai-based charity that rescues, rehabilitates and repatriates victims of human trafficking sold for forced prostitution
www.rescuefoundation.net

Sanlaap – A Calcutta-based charity that aims to protect the human rights of women and girls
www.sanlaapindia.org

The Sun **newspaper** – British newspaper
www.thesun.co.uk

Human Trafficking Web Resource
www.humantrafficking.org

A Global Report on Trafficking in Persons by the United Nations Office on Drugs and Crime (UNODC)
www.unodc.org/unodc/en/human-trafficking/global-report-on-trafficking-in-persons.html

Trafficking in Persons Report 2010
http://www.state.gov/g/tip/rls/tiprpt/2010/

Human Trafficking:
Key Statistics

- Adults and children in forced labour, bonded labour and forced prostitution around the world: **12.3 million**

- Successful trafficking prosecutions in 2009: **4,166**

- Successful prosecutions related to forced labour: **335**

- Victims identified: **49,105**

- Ratio of convicted offenders to victims identified, as a percentage: **8.5**

- Ratio of victims identified to estimated victims, as a percentage: **0.4**

- Prevalence of trafficking victims in the world: **1.8 per 1,000 inhabitants**

- Prevalence of trafficking victims in Asia and the Pacific: **3 per 1,000 inhabitants**

* As of July 2010 the world population was more than 6.8 billion people (based on UN and US Census Bureau figures). The human trafficking statistics are from the US Department of State Trafficking in Persons Report 2010.